A WORLD BANK COUNTRY STUDY

Reducing Poverty in India

Options for More Effective Public Services

The World Bank
Washington, D.C.

World Bank Country Studies are among the many reports originally prepared for internal use as part of the continuing analysis by the Bank of the economic and related conditions of its developing member countries and of its dialogues with the governments. Some of the reports are published in this series with the least possible delay for the use of governments and the academic, business and financial, and development communities. The typescript of this paper therefore has not been prepared in accordance with the procedures appropriate to formal printed texts, and the World Bank accepts no responsibility for errors. Some sources cited in this paper may be informal documents that are not readily available.

The findings, interpretations, and conclusions expressed in this paper are entirely those of the author(s) and should not be attributed in any manner to the World Bank, to its affiliated organizations, or to members of its Board of Executive Directors or the countries they represent. The World Bank does not guarantee the accuracy of the data included in this publication and accepts no responsibility for any consequence of their use. The boundaries, colors, denominations, and other information shown on any map in this volume do not imply on the part of the World Bank Group any judgment on the legal status of any territory or the endorsement or acceptance of such boundaries.

The material in this publication is copyrighted. Requests for permission to reproduce portions of it should be sent to the Office of the Publisher at the address shown in the copyright notice above. The World Bank encourages dissemination of its work and will normally give permission promptly and, when the reproduction is for noncommercial purposes, without asking a fee. Permission to copy portions for classroom use is granted through the Copyright Clearance Center, Inc., Suite 910, 222 Rosewood Drive, Danvers, Massachusetts 01923, U.S.A.

Cover photos: left, "India. Rajasthan," and right, "India," by Curt Carnemark, 1993.

ISSN: 0253-2123

Library of Congress Cataloging-in-Publication Data (CIP) has been requested

Contents

List of tables

List of Boxes

List of Figures

Abstract

The reforms India started in 1991 hold the promise of considerably improving the living standards of the country's 320 million poor. If India is to meet its objectives of sustaining high rates of economic growth with equity, then there should be a much stronger political commitment to accelerate the development of the country's human resources. This would require implementing policies that work to eliminate social exclusion based on income, gender, or caste.

Since the bulk of the required investments to build human capital comes from public rather than private sources in India, and yields many externalities, it is important that poverty-reduction strategies focus public spending on expanding the poor's access to quality education and health care. This is the central finding of this follow-up report.

The report suggests that targeting government spending to primary education, reducing communicable diseases, improving water and sanitation, and reducing household insecurity through public works programs would do most to reduce poverty.

Acknowledgments

This report was prepared by a team led by Zoubida Allaoua. It draws on contributions from Valerie Kozel (Beneficiary assessments from UP and Bihar), Martin Ravallion and Peter Lanjouw (Benefit incidence analysis of spending on anti-poverty programs and primary education), Deon Filmer and Lant Pritchett (Education), Jeffrey Hammer (Health), Gunnar Eskeland (Decentralization), Ravi Srivastava (Panchayats' role in social development), and Rajni Khanna (Review of DPEP literature). Bhaskar Kalimili and Lin Chin assisted with the statistical appendix.

The report benefited from the comments and advice of John Williamson (Chief Economist, South Asia), Dominique van de Walle and Lionel Demery (reviewers for the whole report), Kalanidhi Subbarao (reviewer for the chapter on safety nets), and Marlaine Lockheed (reviewer for the chapter on education). Richard Skolnik (Sector Manager, SASPH) and Salim Habayeb commented on the health chapter. Keith Hinchliffe and Adriaan Verspoor (SASED) commented on the education chapter. The report also benefited from comments of a number of other colleagues within and outside the Bank. Special thanks are also due to Michael Walton (Director, Poverty Board, PREM) and Colin Bruce for their support. The report was prepared under the guidance of Roberto Zagha (Sector Manager) and James Hanson (Economic Advisor). The document benefited from discussions held in June 1998 with officials from Uttar Pradesh, Himachal Pradesh, Rajasthan, and the Central Government.

Arrangements for missions were made by H. Bhawani. The report was desktopped by Lin Chin. Financial support for preparatory work was provided through the Netherlands Poverty Trust Fund and the Swiss Trust Fund.

Abbreviations and Acronyms

AIDS	Acquired Immune Deficiency Syndrome
ANM	Auxiliary Nurse Midwife
APL	Above Poverty Line
APP	Anti-Poverty Program
AWW	Anganwadi Women Worker
BPL	Below Poverty Line
DC	District Collector/Deputy Commissioner
DPEP	District Programme for Elementary Education
DRDA	District Rural Development Authority
DWCRA	Development of Women and Children in Rural Areas
EAS	Employment Assurance Scheme
ECD	Early Child Development
EGS	Employment Guarantee Scheme
FCI	Food Corporation of India
GDP	Gross Domestic Product
HIV	Human Immune Virus
ICDS	Integrated Child Development Services
IRDP	Integrated Rural Development Program
JRY	Jowahar Rojgar Yojana
MOP	Marginal Odds of Participation
MWS	Million Wells Scheme
NAS	National Accounts Statistics
NCAER	National Council of Applied Economic Research
NEP	National Policy on Education
NFHS	National Family Health Survey
NGO	Non-Governmental Organization
NIEPA	National Institute of Educational Planning and Administration
NRY	Nehru Rozgar Yojana
NSAP	National Social Assistance Program
NSS	National Sample Survey
NSSO	National Sample Survey Organization
PDS	Public Distribution System
PHC	Primary Health Center
PRIs	Panchayati Raj Institutions
SC/STs	Scheduled Castes/Scheduled Tribes
SEWA	Self-Employed Women's Association
SHASU	Scheme of Housing and Shelters Upgrade
SHGs	Self-Help Groups
SUWE	Scheme of Urban Wage Employment
TB	Tuberculosis
TLC	Total Literacy Campaign
TPDS	Targeted Public Distribution System
TRYSEM	Training of Rural Youth for Self-Employment
UPBEP	Uttar Pradesh Basic Education Project
WDR	World Development Report

Currency

Currency	Rs/ US$		
	Official	**Unified**	**Market** [a]
Prior to June 1966	4.76		
June 6, 1966, to mid-December 1971	7.50		
Mid-December 1971 to end-June 1972	7.28		
1971-72	7.44		
1972-73	7.71		
1973-74	7.79		
1974-75	7.98		
1975-76	8.65		
1976-77	8.94		
1977-78	8.56		
1978-79	8.21		
1979-80	8.08		
1980-81	7.89		
1981-82	8.93		
1982-83	9.63		
1983-84	10.31		
1984-85	11.89		
1985-86	12.24		
1986-87	12.79		
1987-88	12.97		
1988-89	14.48		
1989-90	16.66		
1990-91	17.95		
1991-92	24.52		
1992-93	26.41		30.65
1993-94		31.36	
1994-95		31.40	
1995-96		33.46	
1996-97		35.50	
1997-98		37.16	
January 1998		39.36	
February 1998		38.91	
March 1998		39.50	

Note: The Indian fiscal year runs from April 1 through March 31.

Source: IMF, International Finance Statistics (IFS), line "rf"; Reserve Bank of India.

---

[a] A dual exchange rate system was created in March 1992, with a free market for about 60 percent of foreign exchange transactions. The exchange rate was reunified at the beginning of March 1993 at the free market rate.

ECONOMIC DEVELOPMENT DATA

GNP Per Capita (US$, 1996-97): 380[a]

Gross Domestic Product (1996-97)

	US$ Bln	% of GDP	Annual Growth Rate (% p.a., constant prices)					
			70-71-75-76	75-76-80-81	80-81-85-86	85-86-91-92	92-93	93-94-96-97
GDP at Factor Cost	323.7	90.0	3.4	4.2	5.4	5.2	5.3	7.1
GDP at Market Prices	359.7	100.0	3.3	4.2	5.6	5.4	5.3	7.0
Gross Domestic Investment	90.7	25.2	5.3	3.7	5.7	6.6	12.3	11.4
Gross Domestic Saving	78.8	21.9	4.4	2.6	4.6	7.9	9.7	12.5
Current Account Balance	-4.7	-1.3	--	--	--	--	--	--

Output, Employment and Productivity (1990-91)

	Value Added		Labor Force [b]		V. A. per Worker	
	US$ Bln.	% of Tot	Mill.	% of Tot.	US$	% of Avg.
Agriculture	82.5	31.0	186.2	66.8	443	46.4
Industry	78.0	29.3	35.5	12.7	2198	230.2
Services	105.7	39.7	57.2	20.5	1848	193.7
Total/ Average	266.2	100.0	278.9	100.0	954	100.0

Government Finance

	General Government [c]			Central Government		
	Rs. Bln.	% of GDP		Rs. Bln.	% of GDP	
	96-97	96-97	90-91-96-97	96-97	96-97	90-91-96-97
Revenue Receipts	2476.1	19.4	19.3	1531.4	12.0	11.5
Revenue Expenditures	2936.8	23.0	23.1	1834.1	14.4	14.9
Revenue Surplus/ Deficit (-)	-460.8	-3.6	-3.8	-302.7	-2.4	-3.4
Capital Expenditures [d]	436.6	3.4	4.3	399.9	3.1	3.7
External Assistance (net) [e]	29.9	0.2	0.6	344.3	2.7	2.3

Money, Credit, and Prices

	90-91	91-92	92-93	93-94	94-95	95-96	96-97
	(Rs. billion outstanding, end of period)						
Money and Quasi Money	2658.3	3170.5	3668.3	4344.1	5314.3	6040.1	7001.8
Bank Credit to Government (net)	1401.9	1582.6	1762.4	2039.2	2224.2	2577.8	2888.2
Bank Credit to Commercial Sector	1717.7	1879.9	2201.4	2377.7	2927.2	3446.5	3753.6
	(percentage or index numbers)						
Money and Quasi Money as % of GDP	49.6	51.4	52.0	53.6	55.2	54.0	54.8
Wholesale Price Index (1981-82 = 100)	182.7	207.8	228.7	247.8	274.7	294.8	314.6
Annual Percentage Changes in:							
Wholesale Price Index	10.3	13.7	10.1	8.4	10.9	7.3	6.7
Bank Credit to Government (net)	19.7	12.9	11.4	15.7	9.1	15.9	12.0
Bank Credit to Commercial Sector	13.2	9.4	17.1	8.0	23.1	17.7	8.9

a. The per capita GNP estimate is at market prices, using World Bank Atlas methodology. Other
   conversions to dollars in this table are at the prevailing average exchange rate for the period covered.

b. Total Labor Force from 1991 Census. Excludes data for Assam and Jammu & Kashmir.

c. Transfers between Centre and States have been netted out.

d. All loans and advances to third parties have been netted out.

e. As recorded in the government budget.

Balance of Payments (US$ Millions)   **Merchandise Exports (Average 1990-91-1996-97)**

	1994-95	1995-96	1996-97
Exports of Goods & NFS	32,990	39,668	42,379
Merchandise, fob	26,855	32,311	33,764
Imports of Goods & NFS	41,437	51,213	54,271
Merchandise, cif	35,904	43,670	48,063
of which Crude Petroleum	3,285	3,442	4,797
of which Petroleum Products	2,396	3,759	5,239
Trade Balance	-9,049	-11,359	-14,299
Non Factor Service (net)	602	-186	2,407
Resource Balance	-8,447	-11,545	-11,892
Net factor Income[a]	-3,711	-3,497	-3,863
Net Transfers[b]	8,093	8,506	11,071
Balance on Current Account	-4,065	-6,536	-4,684
Foreign Investment	4,922	4,794	5,834
Official Grants and Aid	416	345	410
Net Medium & Long Term Capital	1,539	-382	-4,197
Gross Disbursements	6,715	6,641	3,044
Principal Repayments	5,175	7,023	7,240
Other Capital Flows[c]	3,228	-1,169	5,397
Non-Resident Deposits	818	944	3,439
Net Transactions with IMF	-1,174	-1,719	-972
Overall Balance	6,858	-2,004	6,199
Change in Net Reserves	-5,684	3,723	-5,227
Gross Reserves (end of year)[d]	21,160	17,436	22,664

Rate of Exchange

End-Mar 1998[e]	US$ 1.00 = Rs. 39.50

Merchandise Exports (Average 1990-91-1996-97)

	US$ Mil	% of Tot.
Tea	386	1.6
Iron Ore	486	2.1
Chemicals	1,919	8.1
Leather & Leather products	1,457	6.2
Textiles	3,000	12.7
Garments	2,875	12.2
Gems and Jewelry	3,894	16.5
Engineering Goods	3,229	13.7
Others	6,363	26.9
Total [f]	23,610	100.0

External Debt, March 31, 1997

	US$ Mil.
Public & Publicly Guaranteed	74,406
Private Non-Guaranteed	7,382
Total (Including IMF and Short Term)	89,827

Debt Service Ratio for 1996-97

	% curr receipts
Public & Publicly Guaranteed	20.6
Private Non-Guaranteed	1.3
Total (Including IMF and Short Term)	24.5

IBRD/ IDA Lending, March 31, 1997 (US$ Mil)

	IBRD	IDA
Outstanding and Disbursed	8,768	17,616
Undisbursed	3,097	4,368
Outstanding incl. Undisb.	11,865	21,984

-- Not available.

a. Figures given cover all investment income (net). Major payments are interest on foreign loans and charges paid to IMF, and major receipts is interest earned on foreign assets.

b. Figures given include workers' remittances but exclude official grant assistance which is included within official loans and grants, and non-resident deposits which are shown separately.

c. Includes short-term net capital inflow, changes in reserve valuation and other items.

d. Excluding gold.

e. The exchange rate was reunified at the market rate in March 1993.

f. Total exports (commerce); net of crude petroleum exports.

Sources: Natinal Accounts Statistics; Ministry of Commerce; Union Budget Documents;
Reserve Bank of India; 1991 Census;World Bank Debt Reporting System.

India Social Indicators

	Latest single year			Same region/income group	
	1970-75	**1980-85**	**1990-96**	**South Asia**	**Low-income**
POPULATION					
Total population, mid-year (millions)	613.5	765.1	945.1	1,265.8	3,236.2
Growth rate (% annual average)	2.3	2.1	1.8	1.9	1.8
Urban population (% of population)	21.3	24.3	27.1	26.6	29.1
Total fertility rate (births per woman)	5.6	4.4	3.1	3.4	3.2
POVERTY					
(% of population)					
National headcount index	..	..	35.0	..	..
Urban headcount index	..	..	30.5	..	..
Rural headcount index	..	..	36.7	..	..
INCOME					
GNP per capita (US$)	180	280	380	380	490
Consumer price index (1987=100)	45	85	227	233	275
Food price index (1987=100)	..	83	238	..	..
INCOME/CONSUMPTION DISTRIBUTION					
(% of income or consumption)					
Lowest quintile	5.9	..	9.2	..	..
Highest quintile	49.4	..	39.3	..	..
SOCIAL INDICATORS					
Public expenditure					
Health (% of GDP)	..	..	0.7	0.8	1.5
Education (% of GNP)	..	3.4	3.8	3.0	3.6
Social security and welfare (% of GDP)	..	..	..	..	..
Net primary school enrollment rate					
(% of age group)					
Total	..	..	..	..	..
Male	..	..	..	..	..
Female	..	..	..	..	..
Access to safe water					
(% of population)					
Total	31	54	81	78	76
Urban	80	80	85	83	80
Rural	18	47	79	74	72
Immunization rate					
(% under 12 months)					
Measles	..	1	84	82	80
DPT	..	41	86	83	81
Child malnutrition (% under 5 years)	..	..	66	..	..
Life expectancy at birth					
(years)					
Total	50	52	63	62	63
Male	51	52	62	61	62
Female	49	51	63	63	64
Mortality					
Infant (per thousand live births)	132	101	65	73	68
Under 5 (per thousand live births)	202	173	85	93	94
Adult (15-59)					
Male (per 1,000 population)	324	261	229	239	231
Female (per 1,000 population)	353	279	219	230	206
Maternal (per 100,000 live births)	..	460	437	..	..

World Development Indicators 1998 CD-ROM, World Bank.

EXECUTIVE SUMMARY

The reforms India started in 1991 hold the promise of considerably improving the living standards of the country's 320 million poor. The economy has responded well to the reforms, and the government has explicitly committed itself to accelerate the development of the country's human resources. By maintaining its commitment to economic liberalization; redirecting towards infrastructure, health, and basic education the large resources now absorbed by ill-targeted subsidies; and improving the effectiveness and targeting of spending in education, health, and anti-poverty programs, India can give its long battle to reduce poverty a new impetus.

Where does India stand?

In the half century since its independence, India has made many notable social and economic achievements in a democratic political setting: among them, the eradication of famine, the reduction in population growth and the creation of a large pool of technical and scientific talent. It also managed to reduce poverty over that period, but only since about 1975 has the decline become fairly steady, albeit slow. And, although the incidence of poverty has declined from 45 to 36 percent between 1950 and 1993-94, population growth caused the numbers of the poor almost to double in the same period, from 164 million to 320 million. Of that total, more than three out of four (76 percent) live in rural areas.

Where policies have increased growth, particularly agricultural growth, and improved human development (as measured by various indicators), poverty has fallen faster, as indicated in the World Bank's 1997 Poverty Assessment. In contrast, where growth was slow or where human development policies were lacking, ineffective, or misdirected to the politically or economically more advantaged, poverty reduction has been relatively slow. Policies that sustain and accelerate labor-intensive economic growth and raise the poor's health status and education provide them with the skills to take advantage of opportunities for better paying jobs while avoiding the ravages of ill-health. Such policies have worked in other developing countries and in some Indian states.

The central finding of this follow-up report is that the success of education and public health in reaching the poor depends not only on more spending but on improving the quality of service they receive. The importance of effective delivery of education and health is underscored both by qualitative surveys in India's poorest districts in Uttar Pradesh (UP) and Bihar and by a new empirical assessment of the degree to which the poor benefit from public spending on education, health, and anti-poverty programs.

The report suggests that targeting government spending to primary education, reducing communicable diseases, improving water and sanitation, and reducing household insecurity through public works programs would do most to reduce poverty. Early results from the implementation of the Targeted Public Distribution System (TPDS) in UP and Bihar indicate that the poor seem to be benefiting more than the non-poor from the subsidies on foodgrains. If this finding is generalized across India, then targeted foodgrain subsidies could supplement public works programs to reduce household food insecurity.

The face of poverty in India

Being poor in India means lacking the good health and skills to make the most of the economic opportunities growth can open. Over half of India's children under five years of age still suffer from malnutrition and, later in life, from the illnesses to which an ill-nourished childhood exposes those who survive it. Being poor in rural India means, as well, a higher than 50 percent likelihood of being illiterate. In the states of Andhra Pradesh, Bihar, and Rajasthan, barely half the rural men (poor or not) can read; in Rajasthan and Bihar barely a quarter of *all* the women are literate, a percentage that drops to 17 percent in rural Rajasthan and 22 in rural Bihar.

The incidence of poverty and the poor's access to social services varies considerably from state to state and even within states. Poverty in rural Bihar, for instance, was almost twice as widespread (a 58 percent rate of incidence) in 1993-94 as in rural Kerala (31 percent). Even within a single state, the variance can be striking, for example, between rural poverty incidence in southern (68.8) and northern (45.5) Orissa, and inequality is higher within wealthier regions. Similarly, living in Kerala rather than in Bihar made an average child 25 percent more likely to attend school. And the better health status of the poor in Kerala is largely explained by Kerala's better education, water, and sanitation and basic infrastructure services.

Even more noticeable than geographic differences in poverty, social indicators, and regional inequality are the inequalities that persist across gender, caste, and ethnic groups. The size of the gender gap in schooling varies widely across states, but works out to a significant average disadvantage for girls wherever they live and however affluent or disadvantaged their families. Boys all over India are about 20 percent more likely than girls to have finished the 8 years of basic education. Being a poor, pregnant woman means risking death. India's maternal mortality is so high (437 per 100,000) that the nation accounts for one in every four maternal deaths worldwide.

Similarly, members of scheduled castes, particularly their children, are more likely to die prematurely (Chapter 3). What is sadly consistent across states and regions is the higher risk of poverty among women, illiterates, the landless, and members of scheduled castes and tribes.

The differences in reaching the poor and reducing poverty reflect more than natural advantages or disadvantages. They partly mirror conscious decisions (as in Kerala) to improve the poor's health and their education and, consequently, their opportunities to gain a share of economic progress. Kerala has the lowest infant mortality rate and the highest rates of male and female literacy, managing to get almost as high a level of enrollment in primary school for its poorest children (88.7 percent) as for its wealthiest (97.5 percent). Having forgone such investments, Bihar—the poorest among India's 16 largest states—has the lowest level of male literacy, the second lowest level of female literacy, and the sixth highest level of infant mortality.

Are the poor benefiting from public spending?

Public spending on education does not benefit the poor, who either do not send or do not keep their children in school, on an equal footing with the better off, even at the primary level. The evidence in Chapter 2 shows that enrollment and attainment levels of the two social-economic groups differ enormously. Fewer than half the children from poor households enroll and when they do, only one in five of them completes basic education. By contrast, wealthier households do send their children of both sexes to school no matter where they live, and over 80 percent of them complete grade 8. Poor girls, in a brutal contrast that highlights gender barriers, are only one-eighth as likely to complete grade 8 as their female counterparts among the well-to-do. Of course, failure to enter or complete primary education means that the poor also do not benefit from the large subsidies to secondary and tertiary education.

Despite the economic and social returns of primary schooling, approximately 33 million youngsters (out of 105 million) between the ages of 6 and 10 do not attend school, and four in five of those who enroll never complete basic education. It can be presumed that their parents felt that the benefits from schooling, or the costs to undertake it, were not worth the effort. That unfortunate decision is made easier when, as many villagers from UP and Bihar reported, classrooms are too far away or ill-equipped, teachers are absent most of the time and not well qualified, and potential students from disadvantaged social groups are made to feel unwelcome. Poor parents, moreover, are less likely to invest in the education of their daughters because the returns on such investment are seen to accrue to the family into which the daughters marry.

In health, the poor face a disproportionately higher risk than the rich of falling sick, particularly from infectious diseases. They are more likely to lose their children before they reach the age of two. Poor members of scheduled castes run even higher risks of premature death. And because they are less likely to be educated and they must often use shared sources of water and surface water (lakes, streams, ponds) without adequate sanitation facilities, they are dangerously exposed to illness (Chapter 3). Perhaps the most important finding of the research carried out for this report is the failure of India's primary health centers to deliver the care needed to reduce infant mortality. The study could not find any significant correlation between child survival and the availability of public health facilities.

Traditional anti-poverty programs are not compensating for the shortcomings in the fields of education and health. Indeed, they are funneling many of their benefits to the non-poor. According to data from the 1993-94 National Sample Survey (NSS), 76 percent of the wealthiest rural households, for instance, are likely to take advantage of the subsidized prices for food under the Public Distribution System while, at the opposite end of the wealth scale, fewer than 70 percent of the poorest households benefit from food subsidies. The poor do participate in rural public works and to a lesser extent in credit programs (IRDP), but all three schemes (PDS, IRDP, and public works) remain loosely targeted.

Reducing poverty: What could public policy do better?

Since the bulk of the required investments to build human capital comes from public rather than private sources in India, and yields many externalities, it is important that poverty-reduction strategies focus increased public spending on expanding the poor's access to *quality* education and health care. To avoid increasing the already large fiscal deficit, the funding for these needed increases could come from reducing the costly and integrated subsidies that are currently the source of large fiscal imbalances and microeconomic distortions, as discussed in the World Bank's 1997 and 1998 Macroeconomic Updates.

Priority for human capital. The returns on primary education are huge: better family health, smaller family size, and healthier children for educated women, for instance. A mother's primary education may do even more than food subsidies to improve child nutrition. Educated workers can take advantage of growth in demand for labor to raise their productivity and earnings. And because educated parents are more likely to send their children to school, education (even if limited to the primary level) perpetuates the benefits from one generation to the next. It is no coincidence that Kerala has enjoyed the highest levels of both male and female literacy and the

fastest decline in the incidence of poverty over the past 40 years.

If India is to meet its objectives of sustaining high rates of economic growth with equity, then schooling must reach the economically and socially disadvantaged. This would require policies that can expand both the quantity and quality of schooling and that work to eliminate social exclusion based on income, gender or caste. The problems are concentrated in UP, Bihar, Madhya Pradesh, Orissa, Rajasthan, Uttar Pradesh and West Bengal. Notwithstanding the remarkable accomplishments of the District Primary Education Project (DPEP) in increasing enrollment in lower primary education, three-quarters of the 33 million 6- to 10-year-olds in these seven states are still not in school.

The policy prescriptions for bringing the poor children into school are not obvious. Success will depend on much stronger political commitment to educate the children of the poor. There is no question that spending levels on education inputs (teachers, classrooms, textbooks, and instructional material) need to increase. Chapter 2 provides estimates of the resource needs to put all children 6-14 years old in school. That said, the empirical findings in this report and those of other research in India produce a consistent picture that *increased spending alone will not be enough to improve enrollment and attainment of the poor*. Improvement in quality of schooling is crucial to attract poor children to school and retain them there, as shown in Chapter 2. Because the opportunity cost is high for them and their families, poor children would not go to school if they perceive it as a waste of their time.

Improving quality of education needs fundamental reforms to change the incentive framework within which teachers, school officials, bureaucrats, and politicians operate. The accumulated experience under the DPEP, the Lok Jumbish, and the experiences of states such as Kerala and Himachal Pradesh should be analyzed to help provide the information necessary to underpin such deeper educational reforms, particularly in the seven states with the highest incidence of school dropouts or non-enrollment. Interesting findings from recent theoretical and empirical research provide some guidance to reforms that are likely to improve outcomes. Some of these reforms are already underway in many states in India. These include decentralization of control over the provision of schooling to the local areas themselves, direct parental involvement, competition through school choice, and community involvement. Madhya Pradesh, for example, is by far the most advanced in decentralizing school management to local institutions such as the Panchayati Raj Institutions, with a consequent increase in enrollment and retention among children of underprivileged groups.

The process and the potential for bringing education closer to its users and beneficiaries through decentralization has generated significant optimism but also considerable caution. The chief fears reflect concern that decentralization could perpetuate, and quite possibly increase, regional disparities in school quality, and social and economic inequities in access to good schooling. Lowered funding levels for education also might be a problem if local control serves as a pretext for diminishing central responsibility.

Guidance on the choice between the various options and the likelihood of success requires further analysis, however, to understand better what changes would be required to the underlying incentives framework for teachers and officials to perform better. Gradually expanding the DPEP model and collecting appropriate information to assess its impact on educational attainment is essential. Raising quality is not as easy as increasing spending, and therefore a stock-taking exercise of what has worked elsewhere in the world and within India is also needed to inform public policy about the design of an effective educational system.

Effective health programs must complement education in raising the potential productivity of labor to reduce poverty. Yet the research carried out for this report found that the public sector has failed to deliver some of the promised care to India's poor. This raises important issues, and more research is needed to understand fully the factors behind the poor performance. This should constitute a priority research area, because the policy implications would be different if the main reason is poor quality than if it is because of the availability of an easily accessible and large private sector, or both.

Public expenditure on health as currently constituted is likely to have only a limited redistributive impact. Despite its relatively equitable distribution, it is small relative to overall health use and its effects on health outcomes appear to differ greatly from one intervention to another and place to place, especially in its impact on the poor. Chapter 3 of this report identifies four priority areas for increasing the impacts of public spending on the health of the poor, and indeed on the economy in general. *First*, combating communicable disease and expanding public health interventions (see below) would deliver substantial gains from public health spending, particularly for the poor. *Second*, improving access to safe water sources and sanitation facilities and vaccinations would help reduce infant and child mortality and thus reduce fertility and improve maternal health. Because these are activities in which the poor are vastly underserved relative to the non-poor, public interventions in these areas will achieve their biggest impact on the poor. The net cost to the government of extending water and sanitation facilities to poor areas may not be very large, since willingness to pay for these goods is usually quite high and could cover the extension of the system. *Third*, analyses have shown that health education concerning basic hygiene, the value of better nutrition, and preventive care such as public campaigns against tobacco use and for the use of appropriate measures to avoid contracting HIV-AIDS and other sexually transmitted diseases, is an important part of encouraging behavioral changes needed for long-term improvements in health outcomes.

Fourth, because the rural poor must often meet the financial burden of medical emergencies through debt, distress sale of real assets, or reductions in food or other important consumption items, there is merit in subsidizing hospital treatment. The benefit of providing this "in effect" social insurance—on top of the value of the service itself—is in the range of 40 to 70 percent of the costs of providing the service to patients in the lowest 40 percent of the population, people for whom insurance is not a realistic option. Public subsidies to hospital care can thus play an important redistributive role as long as referral systems are reformed to ensure that access is based on need rather than income and social status.

The provision of medical care to the poor as an insurance does not have to be provided only through publicly managed hospitals. The poor could also be served by public financing of private provision of services in rural areas (with an appropriate system of incentives and monitoring); by a major effort to increase the quality of care through training, changes in incentives, and regulations; or by community-based insurance schemes. India's policy makers will need to evaluate the option of subsidizing hospital treatment against other alternatives and choose what services they will subsidize and what type of provision they will promote. Further research is needed, here again, to underpin the necessary reforms to both public and private health systems in India and further guide the policy.

Reforming anti-poverty programs. Public works programs are generally considered to have been relatively successful in reaching the poor. However, the benefit incidence analysis based on data gathered on such programs in the 1993-94 NSS has found that the non-poor benefit fairly significantly from such programs, although less so than under the IRDP or the PDS. The marginal incidence analysis suggests that expanding access of the poor to the public works programs (preferably through reallocation of spending away from the other, less effective poverty programs), while benefiting the poor most, would also reduce the extent to which the non-poor could capture their benefits. The priority would therefore appear to focus on improving the effectiveness of public works through effective targeting to the genuinely needy and making them fiscally sustainable. Effective targeting need not be exclusive targeting. Some level of spill-over to the non-poor is unavoidable if political support for such programs is to be maintained. Such targeting could be done by setting the wage rate at a level which is no higher than the prevailing market wage where the scheme is introduced. Willingness to work at this wage rate would be the only eligibility criterion. The scheme could also be geographically targeted to poor areas and create assets that are of value to poor people in these areas.

In sum, the challenge that India faces in reducing poverty faster and more effectively than it has in the past is enormous. Last year's poverty report concluded that growth accounted for most of the reduction in poverty incidence over 1951-93. Improvements in redistribution (which occurred either through deliberate government policies or independently) achieved their greatest impact by the mid-1960s, but even that was minimal. As shown in last year's report, the gains to the rural poor since 1970 have been due almost entirely to growth. That report also documented the ineffectiveness of the direct poverty programs in raising the living standards of the poor. The benefit incidence analysis in this report confirms that finding. It is clear that there is a need to phase out a number of the anti-poverty programs, as suggested in the Approach Paper to the Ninth Plan, and direct some of the savings to ensure quality education, which the analysis has shown is more effective in reducing poverty over the long-term than various poverty programs. For the poor to take advantage of the new educational opportunities, however, their health status needs to improve, and this calls for allocating public spending where it is expected to deliver the highest gains to the poor: attacking communicable diseases and increasing access of the poor to good-quality water and sanitation facilities. Improved access to basic services will not only make the poor healthier and better educated persons, it will also allow them to contribute to growth through the higher productivity that education and good health bring and raise their level of welfare through higher earnings that both higher productivity and growth would offer. The message for India is therefore clear: fundamental reforms are needed in the way in which the public sector delivers health and education services to the poor, in order to allow them to take advantage of opportunities for raising their living standards that will come with rapid, labor-intensive growth.

CHAPTER 1: POLICIES FOR GROWTH AND POVERTY REDUCTION: THE CHALLENGES AHEAD

Introduction

*C*an India overcome poverty? Although the proportion of poor people below the poverty line in India has dropped from 45 percent in 1950 to 36 percent in 1993-94, the total number of poor has nearly doubled from about 164 million to 320 million. Of these poor people, more than three out of four (76 percent) live in the countryside, where sustained investments in human development and infrastructure have been lacking or ineffective (or misdirected, in the case of many government poverty programs, to the politically or economically more advantaged). Yet it is those investments, as complements to overall economic growth and to agricultural growth in particular, that the World Bank's 1997 Poverty Assessment found to offer the greatest prospect of reducing poverty. The report found that policies which sustain and accelerate labor intensive economic growth and develop the human capital of the poor by raising their levels of health and education offer them opportunities to escape from solely selling their unskilled labor at wages too low to escape poverty. Such policies have worked in other developing countries and, most importantly, in some Indian states (Box 1.1). If recent high rates of growth can be sustained, and with the committed implementation of effective public policies, India can and will shrink its massive rural poverty.

The stage is set for progress. Wherever in India policies to encourage growth and develop human resources and infrastructure have been effectively combined, poverty has diminished rapidly (Box 1.1). *From these results, the lessons for the future are clear.* A more open trade regime since 1991, a significant reduction in distortions, and a liberalized economy with a major role for the private sector have already improved agricultural incentives. They also are creating the conditions for labor-intensive industrialization that will not only enhance the country's growth prospects but also increase the poverty-reducing effects of industrialization and the

> **Box 1.1: Poverty reduction: The primacy of growth and human capital development**
>
> Differing performances in rural poverty reduction were due to both differing initial conditions in human resource development and physical infrastructure and different rates of agricultural growth. For instance, the incidence of poverty in Bihar declined at an annual rate 2.1 percentage points below that in Kerala, but only about half of that differential is explained by the initial conditions. Other factors, particularly the slow growth in agricultural output per hectare, have been important in explaining Bihar's unimpressive performance. It is nonetheless notable that if Bihar had started off with Kerala's level of human resource development in the 1960s, the differential in the rates of poverty reduction between the two states could have been narrowed to less than half their observed levels. Also the implicit trade-offs can be large. For Bihar to overcome the adverse effects of its initially disadvantageous human resource development relative to Kerala would have required that its agricultural yields grew annually at a rate 3.4 percentage points higher than Kerala's. The study's results also suggest that Kerala's low growth rate in farm yields inhibited its rate of poverty reduction. Kerala's trend rate of reduction in the poverty rate would have been 3.1 percent per year, rather than the 2.3 percent it has actually achieved, had it had the same trend growth rates in farm yields as Punjab-Haryana.
>
> *Source*: Datt and Ravallion 1996b.

role of urban areas in this process. Along with the prospects for robust agricultural performance as a result of deregulation, India's recent high rates of growth and its continued integration into the world economy open the way for a concerted effort aimed at maximizing the beneficial impact of the expected future rapid and labor-intensive growth itself on rural poverty and most likely on urban poverty. *But for that effort to bear fruit, investments in human resources are crucial. They are the focus of this report.*

Even in a setting of strong growth, poor women, men, and children must count largely on their own human capital to enable them to participate in and benefit from a private sector-led growth, otherwise they will be left behind. Their access to such social services as health and education is therefore crucial to their prospects for moving permanently out of chronic poverty, and expanding that access is a key component of the long-term strategies for sustained economic growth and poverty reduction (Box 1.2).

This report, after reviewing the profile of the poor (Chapter 1) and their share in the benefits of public spending (Chapters 2, 3, and 4), undertakes a longer-term examination of the prospects for reducing and possibly eliminating persistent chronic poverty through more effective public policies to encourage and sustain rapid and broad-based growth (Chapter 1) and to bolster the human capital of the poor through the provision or pricing of education and health services (Chapters 2 and 3). Recognizing, however, that

---

Box 1.2: The centrality of education to growth and individual and society's welfare

Two overall conclusions can be drawn from the survey of the economic and social outcomes of education. *First*, the economic and social benefits of education are greatest when a critical minimum level of educational attainment has been achieved across the population. Mass expansion of primary education that raises India's currently low educational attainment (averaging about 1.9 years for workers in 1981), to a threshold of about 4 to 5 years of completed primary education per worker, would have high payoffs in economic and social benefits. *Second*, the benefits of education extend beyond individuals who receive schooling directly. Other members of society also gain. The resulting improvements in economic efficiency provide continuing justification for public sector involvement in education. Primary schooling offers the greatest economic and social returns, followed by secondary schooling.

The economic outcomes of education have been estimated using a range of techniques, including aggregate and enterprise-based production functions, and rate of return analysis (a survey is in the World Bank 1997a). All show positive returns to education in India. Some even show higher returns in the 1980s compared with the 1970s, a result of the impact of the timid liberalization in the 1980s (Loh, 1995). Aggregate production functions suggest that a one-year increase in the average education of the work force can raise output by 13 percent and that the increased educational level can contribute around one-quarter of the increase in economic output. Farm-based production functions show that in agriculture, education helps increase output, primarily by increasing the adoption of new technologies and farming practices. In areas where schooling across the farm population has reached a certain threshold, the potential effects of an advance in agricultural technology are more fully realized. Rate of return analysis and earnings functions suggest that private and social returns to education are around 8 to 9 percent with the highest returns registered for lower-caste graduates. The literature on the cost-benefit of education shows that the returns to schooling are very high in developing countries. For example, one extra year of primary education increases a person's future productivity (that is, hourly wage rate) by 20 percent in India (Psacharopoulos 1994 as cited in van der Gaag 1997).

With respect to the social (or nonmarket) outcomes of education, the NFHS shows strong overall relations between educational levels, fertility and infant and child mortality rates, and the nutritional status of children. Primary schooling appears to have a stronger effect on fertility rates than previously thought. Two effects are discernible. *First,* within each state, there is a clear inverse relation between the level of schooling and both the desired and the actual fertility rate. *Second*, in states with higher schooling levels, fertility rates are lower at each level of schooling than in states with lower schooling levels. Lower levels of fertility are also generally judged to have social benefits, particularly in countries such as India that have high rates of population growth. A demographic transition from high to medium or low population growth is widely viewed as important in raising living standards. Expanding primary and secondary education could bring such a demographic transition in India.

The mother's education reduces infant and child mortality, and even a few years of schooling have a positive effect. Here again, there appears to be a wider societal effect that is dependent on a critical threshold of schooling across the population.

These social outcomes have many spill-over efforts. Lower population growth rates substantially reduce the financing required to achieve and maintain universal primary education. Lower child mortality rates reduce suffering, increase female labor force participation rates, and probably play a part in the process through which parents come to desire fewer but healthier children. Healthier, better-fed children tend to achieve more while in school and to become more productive adults. All these outcomes appear to be closely linked to the level of mothers' education.

Source: World Bank 1997a.

transient poverty in poor households due to old age, drought years, disability, death of the breadwinner, or other blows to income will remain an important concern, Chapter 4 proposes a possible framework for erecting effective safety nets.

This report primarily, although not exclusively, addresses rural poverty about which our understanding rests on a much stronger analytical underpinning. While population trends point to a continued rise of the urban sector, current poverty incidence as well as numbers of poor remain considerably higher in rural than in urban areas, which are, moreover, relatively better off in terms of access to and use of publicly provided social services. Nonetheless, the report's analysis and recommendations are still likely to be of much relevance to the urban sector. That said, further analytical research will be undertaken to better inform public policy on how the workings of the urban economy affect the poor and what public policies are needed to improve their welfare.

Poverty incidence: India-wide and by region

India's pervasive poverty, predominantly rural (Table 1.1, Annex 1, Table 1), is mirrored in health, education, and nutrition indicators that remain too low—even accounting for India's low per capita income. Although infant mortality rates, as one example, fell from 146 deaths per thousand births in the 1950s to 80 at the start of this decade, the Indian rate is still one of the highest in the world. Life expectancy at birth, now twice the 30 years that was the Indian average in 1947, remains well below that of China (69 years). In 1993-94 (NSS), adult literacy rates ranging from 42.8 percent to 49 percent were recorded in six (Bihar, UP, Rajasthan, Madhya Pradesh, and Andhra Pradesh) out of India's 16 states. And female literacy rates were much lower: 25.6 percent (Rajasthan), 26.3 (Bihar), 29.7 percent in UP (Annex 1, Table 2). High maternal mortality (437 per 100,000) accounts for a quarter of all maternal deaths on the planet.

Sharp disparities remain between development-oriented states and laggards, between women and men, between adults and children, and between urban and rural areas. The range in poverty reduction among the

Table 1.1: Poverty in India: 1993-94 Estimates based on the Expert Group methodology	Rural	Urban	Total
Head count	37.1	33.2	36.1
Number of poor (mill.)	244.0	76.0	320.0
Percent of total	76.3	23.7	100.0
Poverty gap	8.4	8.4	8.4
Squared poverty gap	2.8	3.1	2.9

Source: Haque, Lanjouw, and Ravallion 1998.

states is so wide that Kerala's progress in lowering the head count index of poverty (2.4 percent per year, on average, between 1957-58 and 1993-94) outpaced Bihar by more than 120 times and Rajasthan by more than four times. Kerala is the top performer overall among the 16 major Indian states—which together accounted for more than 97 percent of India's population in 1991 (Table 1.2). During 1993-94, when Kerala had brought the proportion of its rural population living in absolute poverty down to 25.4 percent, the figure for Bihar (the worst performer and home to 10 percent of India's people) was 58 percent—more than twice as high.

While the relative position of a state is rarely identical across different indicators of well-being, certain regularities appear across the columns of Table 1.2. States such as Bihar, Orissa, UP—a state whose 160 million people outnumber the populations of all but five of the world's nations— Madhya Pradesh, Rajasthan, and to some extent AP (poor social indicators) are nearly always clustered at the low end of the rankings. These states account for more than half of India's population. By contrast, Kerala, Punjab, and Haryana—home to less than 8 percent of India's population—cluster near the top for most indicators.

Even within states, because of wide geographic variations poverty data need to be broken down beyond aggregate levels of incidence. Following similar work (Drèze and Srinivasan 1996) and using the quinquennial NSS surveys which have large enough samples to allow such a disaggregation, a recent study (Haque, Lanjouw, and Ravallion 1998) has separated India into 62 regions based on agro-climatic conditions in order to analyze the incidence of poverty by region for 1993-94 (Table 1.3, Annex 1, Table 3). The observation at the state level that Bihar and Orissa were very poor is strongly supported by the regional data. Of the 10 poorest regions in 1993-94—as in 1987-88—

4 were in either Bihar or Orissa. The regional poverty incidence confirms the particularly deprived positions of rural population in Bihar, UP, and Orissa (north eastern states poverty belt). It also confirms both the variation of poverty incidence within particular states—the rate in UP's Himalayan region is significantly lower than in the state as a whole (Annex 1, Table 3)—and the consistency of intrastate rankings and differences over the six years since 1987-88, during which significant economic reforms were thought by some to be worsening the plight of the poor and raising the incidence of poverty. The broad parallels of the 1993-94 data with the earlier findings indicate, on the contrary, that reform has had no particular negative effect on poverty in any particular region.

Inequality is high within wealthier regions. The different measures of inequality: Gini and Atkinson indices place different emphasis on where individuals are in the distribution on per capita consumption within a region. While the Gini measure is more sensitive to changes in inequality at the middle of the distribution, the Atkinson index gives an indication of the inequality among those with the lowest consumption levels and is therefore more sensitive to changes in inequality at the lower end of distribution. The Atkinson measure shows more inequality the larger is the inequality aversion parameter epsilon. On the basis of this measure, of the 10 regions with highest poverty incidence, Maharashtra Inland Central was the most unequal region, followed by Madhya Pradesh South-West, UP South, UP Central, and Bihar South. West Bengal Himalayan shows the least inequality, followed by Assam Plains West, Orissa South, Bihar Central, and Bihar North (Table 1.3). Of those regions with lowest poverty incidence, AP Coastal was the most unequal region (Atkinson epsilon=2), followed by AP Inland North, AP Inland South, and Maharashtra Coastal. Gujarat Saurashtra was the region with the least inequality. Overall the two different measures of inequality are in broad agreement. The ranking of regions in terms of inequality based on the Atkinson index is confirmed by the Gini index. They confirm again that Bihar is very poor overall. The Atkinson index shows that in Bihar people are equally poor overall (inequality is low both within Bihar and compared with other regions) and there is not much variation among them. There is, in other words, a large population mass at the lower end of the consumption distribution within Bihar and the other regions where poverty is high and inequality low. In contrast, in regions where poverty is low, the Atkinson index

Table 1.2: State rankings on the basis of alternative indicators of well-being, 1993-94							
	Head count index [a]			Life expectancy [b]		Infant	Literacy rates [a]	
	Total	Rural	Urban	Male	Female	mortality [c]	Male	Female
Punjab	16	16	16	13	12	14	8	11
Andhra Pradesh	15	15	14	7	5	8	2	5
Gujarat	14	14	15	6	6	10	11	9
Kerala	13	11	10	14	13	15	16	16
Haryana	12	13	12	11	10	7	9	8
Rajasthan	11	10	11	4	4	4	4	1
Himachal Pradesh	10	12	13	-	-	-	14	14
Karnataka	9	7	7	10	7	9	7	7
Tamil Nadu	8	6	6	9	9	12	12	12
Maharashtra	7	5	4	12	11	13	15	13
West Bengal	6	9	8	8	8	11	10	10
Asssam	5	8	9	-	-	5	13	15
Uttar Pradesh	4	4	5	2	3	3	3	3
Madhya Pradesh	3	3	3	1	1	2	5	4
Orissa	2	2	1	3	2	1	6	6
Bihar	1	1	1	5	-	6	1	2

Notes: a. 1993-94; b. Early 1990s; c. 1995. The ranking is from highest (16) to lowest (1) performance.
Source: Haque, Lanjouw, and Ravallion 1998 and Economic Survey 1996-97.

indicates that there are, within these relatively well-off regions, subgroups with living standards far below the average or median in those distributions.

Even more noticeable than geographic differences in poverty reduction and regional inequality are the inequalities that persist across gender, caste, and ethnic groups. For example, while 80 percent of girls from households in the top 20 percent of population complete the eight years of basic education, only 9.5 percent of those from the poorest 40 percent do (Chapter 2). Similarly, members of scheduled castes, particularly their children, are more likely to die prematurely (Chapter 3).

These differences reflect more than natural advantages or disadvantages. They mirror, instead, conscious decisions (as in Kerala) to invest in the poor, specifically in improving their health and their education and, consequently, their opportunities to gain a share of economic progress. Having forgone such investments, Bihar—the poorest among India's 16 largest states—has the fifth lowest level of male life expectancy, the lowest level of male literacy, the second lowest level of female literacy, and the sixth highest level of infant mortality. Kerala, by contrast, has the lowest infant mortality rate and the highest rates of male and female literacy (Table 1.2).

Who are the poor?

Profiles in poverty: The role of gender, literacy, landownership, employment status, and caste. Rural poverty in India does not wear a uniform face. Many of the poor manage to provide a steady subsistence level of income for themselves and their families. Others, truly destitute, are often without any means of livelihood. Most gained their low socio-economic status as an inheritance and remain prisoners of it because they have little or no land, few productive assets, no knowledge of reading and writing, and ill-nourished bodies which make them prey to frequent illness. At even higher average risk are illiterate rural women, members of a scheduled tribe or caste or of a landless household, and those who depend on wage earnings (Box 1.3).

Social stratification based on caste, ethnicity, and gender impedes mobility of India's poor. From the

village studies it is evident that the lowest castes, in general, remain easily distinguishable from the rest of village society in terms of both their very low material

---

Box 1.3: Who is poor?
Evidence from village studies in UP and Bihar

A typical "poor" household, according to villagers, is one at the low end of the caste hierarchy (most often a member of the Scheduled Castes (SCs) or Scheduled Tribes (STs)). While the SCs and STs households are usually grouped in a separate hamlet at the edge of the village, a few of these families occupy a homestead plot in the village which belongs to their upper-caste employer. Landlessness in terms of lack of access to fertile, well-watered agricultural land was mentioned as a cause and characteristic of poverty in every village. Lack of a homestead plot was said to be particularly grave, since the homeless are often forced to enter into an attached labor agreement with a wealthy household in order to secure a place to live. Attached laborers usually receive a small plot of land (homestead and/or agricultural) and other benefits from their patron, such as access to credit and food during lean periods. In the worst case the attached laborer is further bound to his patron through chronic indebtedness. Debt bondage, though illegal in India, can still be found. In return, the attached laborer must work on the agricultural fields of the patron whenever called upon to do so, usually at a wage that is no more than half the rate for unattached casual labor. When not working for the patron, the attached laborer may work for other employers on a casual basis. Even those who have homestead land are considered poor if they have no source of income other than seasonal casual labor or collection of forest products.

Particularly in areas with high tribal populations, the very poor were often characterized as those who must spend most of the year relying on gathering and selling firewood or fodder for their livelihood. The women and children of these households are often the primary collectors of these products. Contributing in this way to household subsistence deprives these children of educational opportunities that would equip them to break the cycle of poverty. In addition to endangering their lives, collection and sale of forest products adds significantly to the "double burden" of domestic and external responsibilities that all but the wealthiest women must bear. Widows or the abandoned wives of migrant laborers are particularly vulnerable. Particularly if they have small children to support, these women were invariably placed among the "poorest" by interviewees in all the study villages.

Source: Kozel et al., forthcoming.

Table 1.3: Rural poverty by agro-climatic region				
Region	**Head count index**	**Gini coefficient**	**Atkinson coefficient**	
			e=0.5	**e=1.0**
I. Highest incidence of poverty in 1993-94				
Orissa Sth	68.8	0.22	0.04	0.08
Madhya Pradesh Sth/W	67.8	0.29	0.07	0.14
Uttar Pradesh Sth	67.4	0.30	0.08	0.14
Bihar Sth	62.3	0.26	0.06	0.10
Bihar Nth	58.6	0.24	0.05	0.09
West Bengal Himal	58.4	0.15	0.02	0.04
Bihar Cent	53.6	0.23	0.04	0.08
Uttar Pradesh Central	50.2	0.29	0.07	0.12
Assam Plains W	50.0	0.19	0.03	0.06
Maharashtra Inland Cent	49.8	0.38	0.13	0.22
II. Lowest incidence of poverty in 1993-94				
Punjab Nth	7.3	0.28	0.07	0.12
Karnataka Coast/Ghata	9.0	0.28	0.08	0.13
Gujarat Saurashtra	12.2	0.23	0.06	0.10
Andhra Pradesh In Sth	13.0	0.31	0.09	0.15
Andhra Pradesh In Nth	13.9	0.33	0.09	0.16
Karnataka Isle East	14.5	0.27	0.06	0.11
Maharashtra Coast	15.2	0.29	0.07	0.13
Madhya Pradesh North	16.6	0.27	0.06	0.12
Andhra Pradesh Coast	17.1	0.32	0.10	0.16
Punjab Sth	17.4	0.29	0.07	0.12

Source: Haque, Lanjouw, and Ravallion 1998.

well-being and their limited opportunities to improve their living standards (see below). Even when poverty recedes, traditional inequalities largely remain. Paradoxically, in some households where increasing affluence leads to the adoption of higher-caste rituals and customs, women's ability to engage socially and economically outside of the household declines. The small degree of variance in economic inequality both from poor to affluent region and over time cannot disguise the profound effects on the poor of discrimination based on gender and social status.

Escaping poverty: Barriers in UP and Bihar

Rural poor see non-farm employment as route to upward mobility. Interviews with villagers from poor districts in UP and Bihar and from other states indicate that the poor are not generally well placed to take advantage of non-farm employment opportunities likely to lead to better lives (Box 1.4). While better able to list the causes of downward mobility than causes of economic betterment, the villagers did identify household members who had gained employment and a degree of security outside the agricultural sector. In general, upward mobility, when it is observed, usually occurs when a family member finds employment in some regular, salaried, non-agricultural occupation. Although government jobs were particularly sought, good connections—which the poor usually lacked—were required to secure positions other than those reserved for SCs and STs. As part of the gradual transformation of the rural economy, village elites have become more interested in non-agricultural sources of income, so that the poor now face stiffer competition for those non-agricultural sources of income which are available. Non-government jobs outside the village were also mentioned as sources of betterment, with Bihar, in this respect, differing from UP. In Bihar, the movement of migrant laborers to urban areas was said to be so common that it is disrupting family structure and worsening the economic situation of

---

> **Box 1.4: Labor market imperfections and the distributional impact of non-farm employment in India**
>
> Along with a noticeable decline since the mid-1970s in the proportion of the work force employed in agriculture in rural India, non-farm employment has emerged in some places as an important vehicle for poverty alleviation. The trend is driven by two distinct processes. On the one hand, agricultural growth in rural areas and expanding relationships between urban employers and rural workers stimulate non-agricultural activities through various forward and backward linkages. On the other hand, population growth outstripping expansion of cultivable land may push people out of agriculture and into a residual, low-productivity, non-farm sector.
>
> Both processes occur in rural India, but on balance the expanding non-farm sector is more commonly characterized as a dynamic one *pulling* rural workers out of agriculture, than as a residual sector into which the destitute have been *pushed*. However, the degree to which even a dynamic non-farm sector helps the poor depends on the factors which influence access to non-farm incomes. Evidence from detailed studies in Gujarat and Uttar Pradesh suggests that the poor are not generally well placed to take advantages of such new opportunities.
>
> In a study of six villages in Mehsana district, Gujarat, in 1995-96, Unni (1997) examines the influence of individual, household, and community characteristics on the likelihood that an individual would be employed in the non-farm sector, as well as on the earnings of that individual from such employment. She distinguishes between wage and self-employment sources of incomes and finds that both types are associated with higher average incomes than in agriculture. Her findings indicate that *education* is a critical factor influencing both employment opportunities and earnings from non-farm activities. However Unni (1997) identifies several factors which act as impediments to such employment opportunities, even after controlling for the influence of education and a host of other factors. *First*, although female participation rates in the district are generally very high, women are severely underrepresented in the non-farm sector. *Second*, those without a circle of contacts in the non-farm sector seem less well placed to gain access to such employment opportunities. *Finally*, lower-caste villagers are significantly less likely to engage in non-agricultural self-employment activities. Even if they do, they earn considerably less.
>
> A longitudinal study of one village in Moradabad district, Uttar Pradesh, documents the striking expansion of regular non-farm employment opportunities between 1973 and 1993 (Lanjouw and Stern 1997). Employment in, and earnings from, such activities are positively related to education and the number of adult males in the household. They are negatively linked to landholdings. Individuals who belong to the lowest caste in the village not only appear to face higher barriers to access, but also earn significantly less if they do manage to gain entry.
>
> Labor market imperfections thus have seriously weakened the force of the non-farm sector in directly reducing poverty. Even so, the sector is likely to play an important positive (if indirect) role in poverty alleviation by raising wage rates in casual agricultural labor—the sector where many of India's rural poor are concentrated.
>
> *Source:* Lanjouw, and Stern 1997. Unni 1997.

women and children. In the UP study villages migrant labor is less common. In a few cases, though, it is a significant source of income, particularly among Muslims who migrate to the Middle East.

Another path: access to land. Poor households in the other backwards castes (OBCs) in Bihar have begun to move up the economic ladder through shifts to cash crops or animal husbandry. Their experience of investing in agriculture to improve income, however, is more the exception than the rule, largely because the price of agricultural land places its acquisition entirely out of the reach of the rest of the poor landless households. The government has been trying to increase land ownership by redistributing patta lands, but this policy has not been vigorously enforced and the poor have been unable to gain actual possession of lands they own on paper.

Little enthusiasm for education in India, a result of past development strategy and remaining social barriers. Although researchers had expected participants to name education as a source of upward mobility and an avenue to employment, few did. India's past development strategy, which focused on a strategy of capital-intensive industrialization behind closed doors, required skilled labor that few of the poor could provide. And now their children, some of whom have limited primary-level education, have few opportunities outside the farm sector. In some of the

Bihar villages, informants observed that many of the educated poor were unable to find white-collar jobs. These persons were consequently useless to themselves and their families. They refused to work as casual agricultural labor and were therefore unemployed. An important implication of these processes, however, is that more than in the past, the poor stand to gain from reforms that would increase agricultural and non-agricultural productivity, growth, employment opportunities, and hence wages (Box 1.2).

Exposure to risks stemming from ill health or loss of income emerged as one of the most important barriers to escaping poverty. The factors informants described as leading to downward mobility reflected the characteristics of the poor mentioned above. Additionally, forces or events which often drove families into debt and, under the burden of accumulated debts, into poverty included shocks such as a breadwinner's death or disability, expensive illnesses, crop failures, and other natural disasters. Other causes of loss of economic well-being seemed to be related to human fertility, such as the birth of too many daughters, with consequent marriage expenses, and division of lands due to excess sons or separation of the joint family into nuclear units.

Growth and poverty reduction: Policy priorities

The primacy of growth and human capital development. Growth-enhancing public policies, the Bank's 1997 poverty assessment concluded, are the *sine qua non* of lasting progress in reducing poverty. The strongest impetus to poverty alleviation in India has come from economic growth. Economic growth widens economic opportunities, provides the resources needed to invest in human development, and creates the very foundation that will increase its returns—and thus families' willingness to send their children to school, have fewer of them, and treat their girls as they would their boys.

India's overarching development objective during its Ninth Plan period is growth with equity—achieving and sustaining annual rates of growth of 7 to 8 percent and ensuring that this economic progress benefits the poor. The rapid growth of the last few years has shown how much India and the poor stand to gain from a more market-oriented development strategy. The strong economic performance has helped build support across India's political spectrum for the liberalization of the economy. At what speed this will be pursued remains, however, an unresolved—yet critical—issue. The pace will determine the country's growth performance and the potential for poverty reduction.

What needs to be done?

Sustaining growth requires higher and more efficient investments, intensified reform. Since previous country economic memoranda and the 1998 Economic Update have discussed the policy priorities needed to advance the country's development goals, this report will only mention the crucial need for higher investments to raise both India's production possibilities and demand for goods and services and hence ensure rapid reduction of poverty. Increasing the returns of such investments is, however, conditional on further reforms to reduce the country's persistently high fiscal deficits, overcome its tremendous infrastructure problems, improve the efficiency of its financial sector, and liberalize parts of the economy that remain heavily regulated—such as agriculture, small-scale industry, and urban land markets.

What is especially relevant to this report's focus is the fact that the overall growth slowdown in 1997-98 was largely due to a sharp fall (10 percentage points) in agricultural growth. Because the incomes of the poor are so closely associated with the fortunes of the agricultural sector, this chapter concludes by re-emphasizing the need to extend the reforms to unleash productivity growth where, by boosting real rural wages, it has historically contributed most to poverty reduction .

How sustainable is agricultural growth? As the 1990s began, India's agricultural growth was both accelerating and spreading more evenly across states (particularly the eastern, highly populated and high-poverty-incidence states), including rain-fed regions—the result of a remarkable production performance in non-foodgrains, notably oilseeds, and massive investments in rural infrastructure. Evidence indicates, however, that the beneficial impact of exchange rate devaluation and the reduction of manufacturing sector protection that virtually eliminated anti-agricultural bias and improved agricultural terms of trade are no longer sufficient to boost agricultural growth in the short term. The lack of fundamental, structural, agricultural reforms is acting as a brake on the sector's growth potential. Not only is agricultural growth declining in the high-productivity and the historically best-performing states, Punjab and Haryana; it is also deteriorating in states such as West Bengal and UP, where poverty rates are high but where agricultural growth was either strong or improving. The declining performance of foodgrains is also raising additional concerns.

Recent evidence showing the continuation of a 10-or-more-year declining trend in total factor productivity (a measure of technical change) indicates that technological change, the long-term source of rapid agricultural growth, is being eroded. As a consequence long-term prospects for agricultural growth and the scope for higher agricultural wages and returns from family farming are shrinking, and so will rural off-farm employment opportunities. Consistent with this observation, during the 1990s real rural wages fell or stagnated in seven major states (AP, Bihar, Gujarat, Karnataka, Rajasthan, UP, and West Bengal) and grew at a much slower rate in another four states (Haryana, Maharashtra, Orissa, and Punjab).

These worrying signals indicate an urgent need for policy reforms to turn agricultural performance around. Public resources spent on non-targeted subsidies for power, water, and fertilizer are not only the main source of India's large fiscal imbalances; they also contribute to costly resources misallocation and inefficiencies that often extend well beyond the agricultural sector. In their place, growth-enhancing public expenditure programs can reverse declining productivity growth. Strong empirical evidence shows that public investments in rural infrastructure (roads, canal irrigation, and electrification), rural services (deregulated markets and commercial banking), and human capital (education and health) encourage private

investment and production in agriculture. These same studies also indicate that private and public, domestic and foreign, technology development and dissemination; rural infrastructure; irrigation; and human capital are the major determinants of (total factor) productivity growth in Indian agriculture (World Bank 1996).

Poverty reduction depends heavily on such productivity-enhancing investment policies as well as on public investment in rural infrastructure and human capital that would boost the non-farm economy and enhance productivity in agriculture. Falling rice and wheat prices during the 1980s contributed significantly to the rise in the real rural wage (goods) and therefore to the reduction in poverty. A more open trade regime, fewer biases against agriculture, and fast-rising domestic and external demands for Indian agricultural products make the prospects of falling agricultural prices in real terms quite remote. Productivity growth, accordingly, assumes even greater importance in raising real rural wages.

Market deregulation would set the stage for potentially large gains in agricultural efficiency by providing the basis for ending subsidies and instituting growth-enhancing public spending in agriculture. Future liberalization needs to focus in particular on the deregulation of agriculture and of small-scale industries—areas which offer livelihood to many of the poor (Box 1.5). Intimately related to such liberalization is the deregulation of domestic trade, so as to eliminate discrimination against domestic producers and processing, and of the agro-processing industry, important segments of which are still shackled by licensing requirements or scale limitations that impose large costs on activities which should benefit from economies of scale. Liberalization of agricultural policies would not only have positive growth effects, it would also help reduce poverty—two compelling reasons for crucial, urgent action. The forthcoming Rural Development Report recommends actions on which to base a new growth-enhancing strategy for the agricultural sector and for poverty reduction.

Box 1.5: Will deregulation of food processing industry help the poor?

Food doesn't command as much attention from economic planners as high-tech industries do. And nationalists protest that the country doesn't need foreign expertise in food. India's agricultural output is US$65 billion a year and accounts for a third of the country's gross domestic product. So experts say food processing will create many more jobs, especially in rural areas, home to 70 percent of Indians. They also note that food processing is a technology-based industry, a fact they say Indian policy makers overlook. PepsiCo unit Pepsi Foods Ltd. offers a case in point. Five years ago, it set up a research farm in the northern state of Punjab to develop high-yield tomato plants. It contracted farmers to grow the tomatoes, helping 1,200 growers more than triple their output to 32 metric tons an acre. Partly thanks to Pepsi's improvements, Punjab's tomato production in 1994 reached 130,000 metric tons, up from 25,000 tons in 1990.

American food giants recognize that Indian agrobusiness has lots of room to grow, especially in food processing. India processes a minuscule 1 percent of the food it grows, compared with 70 percent for the U.S., Brazil, and the Philippines. A third of all Indian produce is wasted because of poor distribution and storage facilities. But improvements don't come cheap. Raising India's capacity to process fruit and vegetables to just 15 percent of output will require investment of US$3 to US$6 billion, according to McKinsey & Co. Much of this money will have to come from abroad. To continue attracting foreign companies, India's food industry must overcome several high hurdles, including poor roads and licensing requirements or scale limitations that impose large costs on activities which should benefit from economies of scale.

Source: An extract from an article by Miriam Jordan. Reprinted by permission of *The Wall Street Journal* @ 1996 Dow Jones & Company, Inc. All rights reserved worldwide.

Given the challenges that India has previously met and mastered and the foundation being laid through economic liberalization for faster growth, it is altogether possible that India can reduce poverty in the future more rapidly and more effectively than it has in the past. To ensure such progress, as the Bank's 1997 poverty assessment also concluded, the challenge of poverty reduction must remain at the forefront of official concern and become the subject of the same imaginative, thorough, change-minded actions as the country's experiments in stabilization and structural adjustment. Public policy and investments, at the same time, need to concentrate on improving the provision of infrastructure and social services to the underprivileged. Financing for such programs can come from cutting the large share of resources now absorbed by input subsidies to agriculture, and from eliminating existing, ineffective poverty programs. Among the areas most in need of reform and added investment are efforts meant to raise the human capital of the poor. That priority is the focus of the rest of this report.

No long-term strategy for assuring sustained economic growth and reducing poverty can slight the contributions of education and health services to strengthening a nation's human capital and improving equity. Poor people can try many escape routes from poverty, but without the support of reliable health care and access to good schooling, their chances of breaking out of poverty are slim.

The relation between education—whether primary, secondary, or higher—growth, and well-being in development is too obvious to be a subject of debate (Box 1.2). A mother's primary education may do even more than food subsidies to improve child nutrition (Alderman et al. 1992, Sen and Sengupta 1983). Educated workers can take advantage of technological change to raise their productivity and earnings. And because educated parents are more likely to send their children to school, education (even if limited to the primary level) perpetuates the benefits from one generation to the next.

For the estimated 33 million Indian children aged between 6 and 10 who are out of school, to take one striking example, the future is far bleaker than for the 72 million of their contemporaries who are in class. So is the future of a nation that forgoes many of the huge returns that primary education pays: better family health, smaller family size and healthier children for educated women, for instance. Against this certainty, however, stand disturbing trends in India's performance in this vital field. Because the poor who either do not send or do not keep their children in school are not benefiting from public spending on education on an equal footing with the better-off, enrollment and attainment levels of the two groups differ enormously. Fewer than half the children from poor households enroll and when they do, only one in five of them completes the eight-year cycle of basic education. By contrast, wealthier households do send their children of both sexes to school, no matter where they live, and over 80 percent of them complete grade 8. Poor girls, in a brutal contrast that highlights gender

barriers, are only one-eighth as likely to complete grade 8 as their female counterparts among the well-to-do. Among the most disadvantaged social groups, the ratios are even worse: literacy rates of just 19 percent among scheduled-caste women and 46 percent for men. And where poverty is deepest, female literacy is exceptionally low. In general, where social indicators reflect little progress, poverty has also been very slow to decline.

Different states perform differently, both on the education front and in poverty reduction, depending on the policies they pursue to promote school quality and to ease access to school for the poor and for girls. Though it is an essential requirement, the analysis found that it is clearly not enough to have a school physically present if the goal is to bring poor children into classrooms and keep them there for a full cycle. Realizing that goal requires overcoming obstacles of social norms based on caste, gender, and poor quality of teaching, to bring enrollment levels of poor children closer to those of the rich. Unless it shrinks these gaps and assures its poorest girls and boys entry and a full stay in primary and secondary classrooms, India is unlikely to sustain rapid growth and reduce poverty. Nor is it likely to improve the general well-being of its population.

In addition to using data from the 1993-94 NSS data on school enrollment, this chapter focuses on information from the unique database of the National Family Health Survey (NFHS) to explore the factors behind the wide, income-related gaps in enrollment and achievement (see Annex 2). The chapter focuses on long-term policies to reduce poverty and thus does not address short-term issues of reducing adult illiteracy. This chapter builds on the extensive analysis contained in *Primary Education in India* (World Bank 1997a) and extends that analysis in two important respects. *First*, by using the NFHS household survey data, which contain data on well-being (asset ownership) as well as school attendance, the chapter provides for the first time a direct relationship between poverty, gender, and enrollment and attainment gaps across India's income groups and states. *Second*, the analysis extends to the whole eight-year basic education cycle, completing the analysis in the book which focused on the first five years of elementary education.

How much do the poor benefit from public spending on education?

Table 2.1 shows that average primary school enrollment rates for children aged five to nine years tend to be lowest for the poorest quintile, and to increase as consumption per person increases. The average odds of enrollment thus suggest that subsidies (the cost of providing primary education services) to primary schooling would mildly favor the non-poor but that conclusion is reversed with marginal rates of enrollment (MOE)—which are more relevant for determining public spending (see Annex 4.1 for details of calculations of MOE). The MOE fall sharply with rising expenditure (Table 2.2). Note that the calculated enrollment rates from the NSS are appreciably lower than those obtained from schools themselves on which official enrollment rates are based. The official primary enrollment rate for India was over 100 percent in 1993. There are differences in definition. For example, confining the analysis to the age group five to nine misses late starters. However, there are reasons to believe that biases in official sources lead to overestimation of enrollments in India (Kingdon 1996, World Bank 1997a, Drèze and Sen 1996).

Current subsidies to primary education are about as pro-poor and inclusive as the best-targeted,

most effective of the programs directed explicitly at fighting poverty and gender discrimination. The benefit incidence analysis for subsidies to primary education show that the poor would benefit disproportionately more from an increase in spending on primary education (particularly in that spending which would improve school performance) than what the average incidence would suggest. While the average rates of enrollment in Table 2.1 suggest that the share of the total subsidy going to the poorest quintile is only 14 percent (0.71 times one-fifth), the marginal rates in Table 2.2 imply that the poorest quintile would obtain about 22 percent (1.10 times one-fifth) of an increase in the total subsidy going to primary education. And while the average odds of poor children being in school are higher for boys (0.75 versus 0.66), the marginal odds are almost identical (1.09 versus 1.08).

How does the distribution of public spending affect educational outcomes?

Combining education attainment data with indicators of economic status (Table 2.3) helps show the ties between achievement and household economic status and the variances from state to state. While the all India population weighted average is only 68 percent, the proportion of 6- to 14-year-olds reported as being "in school" is lower than the national average in Bihar (51 percent), Rajasthan (59 percent), UP (61 percent), Madhya Pradesh (63 percent), and AP (64 percent). It is near the national average in states like West Bengal (68 percent) and Orissa (69 percent) and much higher than the national average in states like Kerala (95 percent), Tamil Nadu (83 percent), and the Punjab (81 percent).

Table 2.1: Average primary school enrollment in rural India						
Quintile	Boys		Girls		Total	
	Enrollment rate (%)	Average odds of enrollment (mean=1.0)	Enrollment rate (%)	Average odds of enrollment (mean=1.0)	Enrollment rate (%)	Average odds of enrollment (mean=1.0)
Poorest	42.6	0.75	31.6	0.66	37.2	0.71
2nd	53.4	0.93	43.1	0.91	48.6	0.90
3rd	60.5	1.07	50.3	1.06	55.8	1.08
4th	66.1	1.16	58.6	1.26	62.6	1.21
5th	69.9	1.23	65.2	1.38	67.7	1.31

Source: (Lanjouw and Ravallion 1998). The table gives the average primary school enrollment rates as a percentage of children aged five to nine, and the odds of enrollment, defined as the ratio of the quintile-specific enrollment rate to the overall mean. Calculations based on the 1993-94 NSS.

These varying enrollment rates reflect a 44 percentage point higher likelihood that a child aged between 6 and 14 from a rich, rather than a poor, household will be in school. The availability of a comparable wealth index (Annex 2) across states allows a comparison of enrollment rates for rich and poor and of the gaps between them. Column 2 of table 2.3 shows that only half the children from poor households are enrolled, compared to 94 percent of children from better-off households.

As with average enrollment rates, there are very few differences across states in the enrollment of the better-off. For the richest 20 percent, enrollment is uniformly high: above 90 percent in nearly every state. In contrast, comparable rates for children in the poorest 40 percent of Indian households vary widely across states (Table 2.3). Whereas children in the top income bracket in Kerala and UP have nearly identical chances of being at school—98 and 94 percent, respectively—children from poor Keralan households are almost twice as likely—89 percent—to be in classrooms as those of the same economic status in UP (48 percent).

These aggregate figures do not distinguish between children who never enrolled and those who drop out of school. To gain insights into recent (if not current) school going, the analysis uses the experience of a cohort of 15- to 19-year-olds at the time of the

Table 2.2: Marginal odds of primary school enrollment			
Quintile	Boys	Girls	Total
Poorest	1.09	1.08	1.10
	(6.90)	(9.65)	(8.99)
2nd	0.91	0.91	0.97
	(6.05)	(6.99)	(7.92)
3rd	0.92	0.84	0.87
	(5.85)	(6.54)	(7.65)
4th	0.66	0.66	0.67
	(4.10)	(4.28)	(4.77)
5th	0.53	0.70	0.67
	(4.08)	(5.53)	(5.69)

Note: T-ratios between percentages.
Source: Haque, Lanjouw, and Ravallion 1998.

survey, most of whom had largely completed their schooling (Figure 2.1), to draw a profile of attainment according to location and economic status. In AP, for example, 97 percent of the 15- to 19-year-olds from rich households completed grade one, but only 39 percent of those from poor households did so. Over 6 out of 10, in other words, either never crossed the threshold of a classroom or left without finishing their first year. In contrast, 86 percent of the children from rich households—as opposed to only 16 percent of poor children—completed grade 8, the end of the cycle of basic education. Not only did poor children not begin school as often, they were also more likely to leave before completing either primary or basic education (Table 2.4).

Table 2.3: Proportion of 6- to 14-year-olds who are currently "in school," by economic group				
(percent)				
State	Average	Bottom 40 percent	Middle 40 percent	Top 20 percent	Wealth gap (top - bottom)
Andhra Pradesh	63.9	45.7	70.1	91.7	46.0
Arunachal Pradesh	71.1	58.5	77.2	86.5	27.9
Assam	70.3	61.5	86.6	84.6	23.1
Bihar	51.4	37.8	70.7	94.2	56.4
Delhi	87.2	47.7	72.3	92.4	44.8
Gujarat	75.7	55.2	77.1	96.2	41.0
Goa	93.7	77.4	93.1	97.3	20.0
Himachal Pradesh	90.8	72.4	91.3	97.0	24.6
Haryana	81.3	60.5	78.9	95.7	35.2
Jammu	85.7	66.6	86.8	97.9	31.3
Karnataka	70.8	50.7	75.8	94.3	43.7
Kerala	94.9	88.7	96.1	97.5	8.8
Meghalaya	74.9	60.1	81.7	95.9	35.8
Maharashtra	82.0	67.1	83.9	96.2	29.0
Manipur	90.2	80.4	93.9	99.1	18.6
Madhya Pradesh	62.6	46.1	74.4	93.7	47.6
Mizoram	90.7	76.8	93.8	97.4	20.5
Nagaland	89.6	82.4	90.2	98.0	15.7
Orissa	69.7	55.2	86.2	96.9	41.6
Punjab	80.8	42.7	76.8	95.7	53.1
Rajasthan	59.3	41.4	65.4	91.0	49.6
Tamil Nadu	82.5	71.7	85.9	95.0	23.2
Tripura	79.5	71.0	86.9	87.3	16.3
Uttar Pradesh	61.4	48.4	69.3	93.9	45.5
West Bengal	67.8	52.7	82.2	90.2	37.5
All India	67.7	50.0	76.7	94.2	44.2

Source: Filmer and Pritchett 1998. Calculated from NFHS data, 1992-93.

Figure 2.1: Attainment profiles for 15- to 19-year-olds by economic group

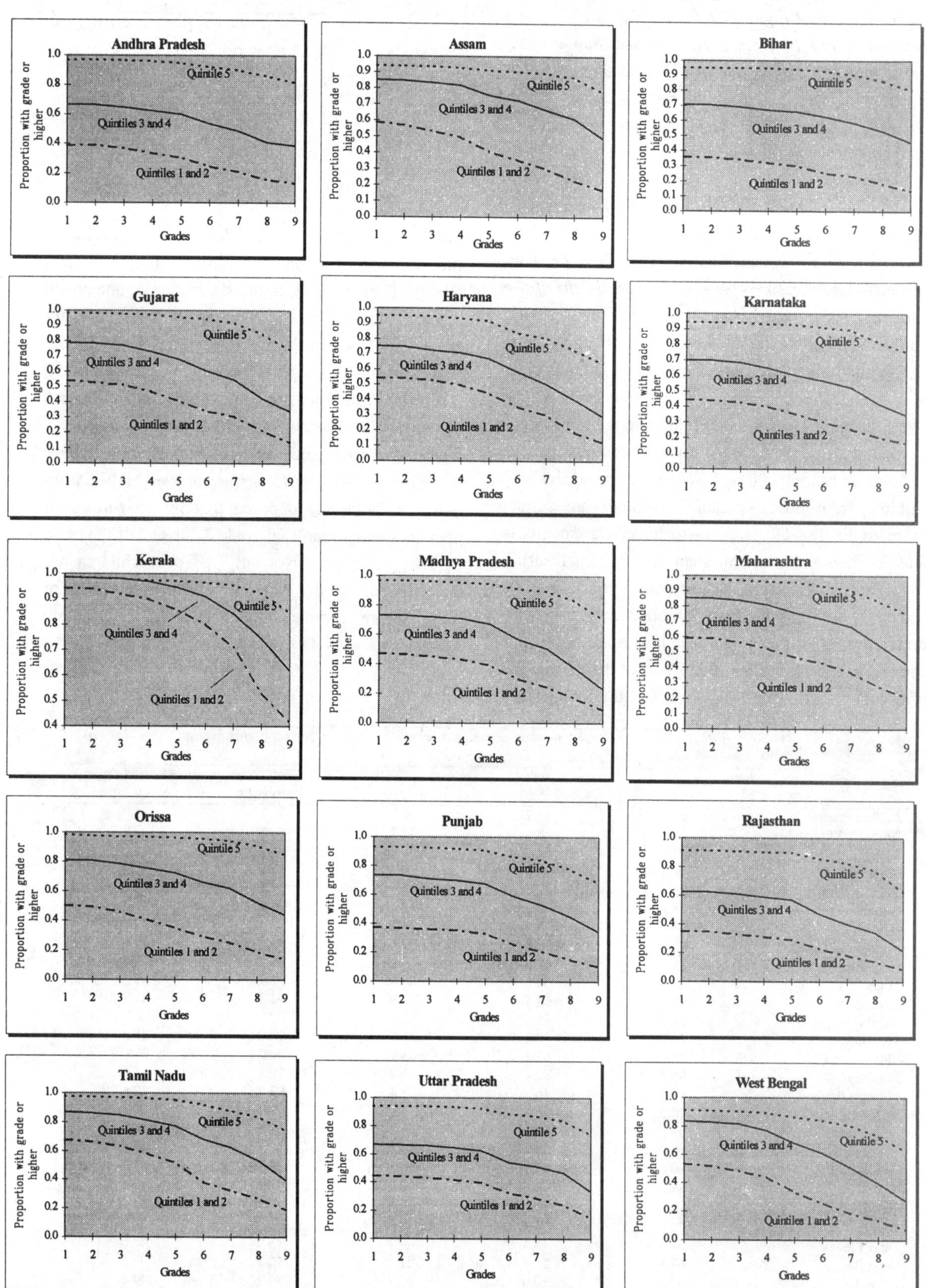

Source: Filmer and Pritchett 1998. Calculated from NFHS data, 1992-93.

As in the rich-poor educational gaps, the size of the gender gap in schooling varies widely across states, but works out—even with such differences—to a significant average disadvantage for girls wherever they live and however affluent or disadvantaged their families. As Table 2.5 indicates, boys all over India are about 20 percent more likely than girls to have finished grade 8. That average is exceeded substantially in AP, Bihar, Haryana, Karnataka, Maharashtra, Madhya Pradesh, Orissa, Rajasthan, and UP. The gap is narrower, on the other hand, in Tamil Nadu (14), West Bengal (11), Himachal Pradesh (12), and Goa (8), and there is actually a slight female advantage in Delhi, Kerala, and the small states of Meghalaya, Mizoram, and Nagaland.

For the poor, however, the gender gap is wider than for the rich. Only 9.5 percent of the daughters in disadvantaged households complete grade 8, compared with 31 percent of the boys (Table 2.5). That 21.5 percent difference all but vanishes in the top 20 percent of households, where 85 percent of boys and 80 percent of girls complete grade 8. While between rich and poor children the average gap in the group who complete basic education is 62 points, rich girls are even further ahead of poor ones—by a staggering 70.5 percentage points. Among boys the discrepancy is 54 points.

Looking at success rates in bringing youngsters through the grade 5 and comparing those levels of achievement to the incidence of poverty still highlights wide differences from state to state. For instance, Tamil Nadu (37 percent) and Rajasthan (43) are similar in the percentage of their households falling into the India-wide bottom 40 percent, but where almost three-fourths of the enrolled finish grade 5 in Tamil Nadu (74 percent), only a little more than half (52 percent) manage to do so in Rajasthan (Table 2.4). And while 52 percent of children from the bottom 40 percent of the population in Tamil Nadu and 53 percent in Himachal Pradesh finished grade 5, in Rajasthan, however, only 29 percent get that far. No such disproportions affect the rich in those states or elsewhere. Grade 5 attainment rates for them are 96 percent in Tamil Nadu versus 90 percent in Rajasthan,

Table 2.4: Simulated flow of 100 children through elementary schooling, by economic group											
	All				Bottom 40 percent				Top 20 percent		
	Cohort	Finished grade 1	Finished grade 5	Finished grade 8	Cohort	Finished grade 1	Finished grade 5	Finished grade 8	Cohort	Finished grade 1	Finished grade 5	Finished grade 8
AP	100	63	57	42	100	38	31	16	100	97	95	86
Arunachal Pradesh	100	75	60	34	100	64	44	18	100	79		58
Assam	100	72	58	42	100	59	41	23	100	94	91	87
Bihar	100	54	50	38	100	36	30	18	100	95	94	86
Delhi	100	88	85	68	100				100	93	91	77
Goa	100	95	89	70	100	77	62	34	100	99	97	85
Gujarat	100	79	70	50	100	54	41	21	100	98	96	84
Haryana	100	79	72	48	100	54	44	19	100	95	92	73
Himachal Pradesh	100	88	84	56	100	63	53	23	100	97	95	82
Jammu	100	83	78	54	100	57	50	20	100	97	94	83
Karnataka	100	69	61	45	100	44	35	20	100	95	93	82
Kerala	100	98	94	75	100	94	86	53	100	99	97	92
Madhya Pradesh	100	66	60	37	100	47	39	17	100	97	95	83
Maharashtra	100	83	75	58	100	59	47	28	100	98	96	83
Manipur	100	90	81	61	100	79	64	36	100		98	93
Meghalaya	100	74	57	33	100	53	34	15	100	97	87	67
Mizoram	100	98	86	57	100	92	57	19	100	99	95	84
Nagaland	100	92	85	57	100	87	71	35	100	96		86
Orissa	100	67	56	40	100	50	35	19	100	98	96	91
Punjab	100	79	75	57	100	38	33	15	100	93	91	78
Rajasthan	100	57	52	34	100	35	29	14	100	91	90	77
Tamil Nadu	100	83	74	52	100	68	52	27	100	98	96	84
Tripura	100	88	71	40	100	78	54	19	100	95		79
UP	100	61	57	42	100	44	40	24	100	94	92	84
West Bengal	100	72	56	34	100	53	34	14	100	91	86	73
All India	100	70	62	45	100	47	38	20	100	96	93	82

Source: Filmer and Pritchett 1998. Calculated from NFHS data, 1992-93.

an insignificant margin. Indeed, nearly every state recorded above 90 percent of the rich as reaching grade 5. For the poor, however, the range of such achievement varied widely, from a high of 86 percent in Kerala to about a third of poor children in AP, Punjab, Orissa, West Bengal, and Bihar.

What causes such gaps in enrollment and achievements?

The causes of this large difference can be found in the varying degrees of school access and retention for the poor across India's states. *State poverty incidence alone does not explain these gaps in educational enrollments and attainments.* Tamil Nadu and Himachal Pradesh for example are much poorer than Andhra Pradesh (head count index basis), yet they have been more effective in reaching a significant share of the poor and bringing them into the educational system. Recognizing that both demand and supply side factors are behind these differentials, successful states such as Himachal Pradesh implemented policies aimed at both expanding the number of classrooms and lowering the social barriers and cost to the poor of sending their children to school.

On the demand side, household behavior and the social and economic characteristics of the household help explain the overall gaps as well as the gender gaps. Poor parents prefer to educate sons: they value a son's education for its effects on his earning potential and on the family's future status. And even if education is not thought of as reducing a daughter's marriage prospects, poor parents are in general less likely to invest in the education of their daughters because the returns on such investment are expected to accrue to the daughters' in-laws. Also affecting household decisions on schooling is the opportunity cost of children's time, which appears to be higher for girls; surveys suggest that girls spend 15-30 percent more time working than boys do. While the main reason given for girls not enrolling or dropping out was domestic work, for boys it is more parents' inability to pay for school expenses. Few rural Indian parents can afford the direct and indirect costs of sending their children to school. Empirical evidence on these costs

Table 2.5: Gender gaps in the proportion of 15- to 19-year-olds who have completed grade 8, by economic group
(percent)

State	All quintiles			Bottom 40 percent			Top 20 percent		
	Male	Female	Gender gap	Male	Female	Gender gap	Male	Female	Gender gap
Andhra Pradesh	52.0	32.8	19.2	25.4	7.2	18.1	90.6	82.0	8.6
Arunachal Pradesh	39.6	28.3	11.3	22.2	15.0	7.3	..	..	..
Assam	47.0	37.4	9.6	28.0	18.3	9.7	90.4	81.9	8.5
Bihar	51.6	25.7	25.9	31.8	6.5	25.3	87.5	85.1	2.5
Delhi	66.9	70.5	-3.6	..	..	..	75.1	78.4	-3.3
Gujarat	57.5	43.0	14.5	30.9	10.0	20.9	88.7	80.4	8.3
Goa	74.5	65.9	8.6	45.8	22.9	22.9	87.0	82.5	4.5
Himachal Pradesh	62.7	50.6	12.1	..	13.6	..	82.8	80.8	2.0
Haryana	56.3	37.9	18.4	30.3	5.6	24.6	74.1	71.5	2.6
Jammu	62.0	45.6	16.4	29.0	8.9	20.1	84.4	81.9	2.5
Karnataka	54.8	35.5	19.3	33.2	9.8	23.4	83.6	79.7	3.9
Kerala	72.8	76.8	-4.0	47.4	57.9	-10.5	90.9	93.7	-2.8
Meghalaya	32.2	33.0	-0.8	16.7	13.3	3.4	..	..	..
Maharashtra	67.2	49.0	18.3	42.1	13.8	28.3	87.0	79.9	7.1
Manipur	62.2	59.9	2.3	39.2	31.7	7.5	87.8	95.9	-8.2
Madhya Pradesh	46.5	25.1	21.4	27.4	5.3	22.1	87.3	78.8	8.5
Mizoram	53.8	59.6	-5.8	18.9	19.1	-0.3	84.6	84.3	0.3
Nagaland	57.0	57.3	-0.3	43.9	29.3	14.6	81.8	89.6	-7.7
Orissa	50.0	29.7	20.3	29.6	9.5	20.1	93.3	88.1	5.2
Punjab	57.2	57.0	0.3	19.3	8.9	10.4	78.2	77.3	0.9
Rajasthan	47.2	19.3	27.9	24.6	1.7	23.0	82.6	71.0	11.6
Tamil Nadu	59.2	45.3	13.9	37.9	17.7	20.2	85.9	82.1	3.8
Tripura	43.9	35.4	8.5	21.2	16.5	4.7	..	..	..
Uttar Pradesh	54.5	29.6	24.9	37.4	8.1	29.4	84.7	82.6	2.1
West Bengal	39.4	28.4	11.0	18.4	9.4	9.1	83.8	64.8	19.1
All India	53.7	35.5	18.2	31.3	9.5	21.8	85.2	79.6	5.6

Note: Cells are empty if there are fewer than 40 individuals from which to calculate the quantity.
Source: Filmer and Prichett 1998.

is limited, but in general, not counting the forgone labor, a household could spend up to Rs. 400 a year to send a child to school (World Bank 1997a).

School quality also affects household behavior and children's motivation to learn. Since primary school attendance is a prerequisite for the higher levels of education to which the children of the rich can and do aspire, they will respond to low public school quality not by dropping out, but rather by getting tutoring and other private preparations for the necessary promotional examinations. Poor children, however, who rarely have expectations for education beyond the first eight grades, value primary school for its own sake, for what learning it might actually impart, not as a gatekeeper determining access to higher levels. Where this is the attitude and where quality of teaching is so low that children learn very little, poor parents, on the other hand, are likely to respond by withdrawing their children from school rather than transferring them to other schools. Improving quality, in other words, is not just a way of boosting the achievement of those already in school but a powerful lever for increasing enrollments of the poor.

These demand-side considerations seem to have a relatively larger effect on poor household decisions to enroll their children, particularly their daughters, and keep them in school than the mere availability of a school. In addition to its household-level survey, the NFHS questioned informants about the availability of primary, middle, and secondary schools in the rural villages studied. For a child in an Indian village, the probability of being in school increases by 11 percent if he belongs to the second rather than the poorest quintile. In contrast, that probability shrinks to 4 percent if he belongs to the poorest quintile and if there is a school in his village. The importance of school availability to enrollment of the poor (when comparing a village having various levels of schools with a village having no schools) was found to be significant in only five states (Karnataka, Madhya Pradesh, Orissa, and UP), whereas income of household was an important determinant of school enrollment in all but three states. Since only about 17 percent of villages in the NFHS sample reported lacking a school and since availability generates only an estimated 4 percent incremental rise in enrollment, expanding the number of villages with school buildings without improving significantly the quality of teaching will not be enough to expand enrollment rates of poor children.

This is not surprising, since there is ample evidence to show that the presence of a school in a village is no guarantee of the genuine availability of education. *First*, schools may be dysfunctional (World Bank 1997a, Drèze et al. 1996) because of high teacher absenteeism (Box 2.1), diversion of physical facility to other uses, and absence of minimum materials such as textbooks, tables, and chairs. *Second*, social barriers may hinder universal availability. Parents may judge single-sex schools facilities and all-male faculties not appropriate for their daughters. Other social barriers, such as caste or income, also play a role in blocking school access to individual children who are made to feel directly or indirectly unwelcome. Teaching practices that discriminate against girls and communicate lower expectations for them than for boys also contribute to the gender gap. So do families' and communities' negative perceptions of the role of education for women. The Lok Jumbish Project has successfully focused on eliminating these perceptions to raise girls enrollment (see for more details Lok Jumbish 1998 and World Bank 1997a, Chapter 5).

According to Indian researchers' findings (World Bank 1997a, pp.134–138), overt discrimination against scheduled castes, while declining, still occurs in primary schools where children are required to sit separately in one corner of the classroom or at the door

Box 2.1: Availability of government primary schools: Community perceptions from UP	
Bikar	Two-thirds are satisfied with the school's performance. Female teachers are on time.
Sandwa	Only one-third satisfied due to high absenteeism. Teachers (who commute from the city) are absent or arrive late and leave early most times..
Hathigan	The school is closed for most days, including the day of the interviewers visit.
Taraon	About two-fifths satisfied. The school is new, but the teacher commutes from the city (30 km) and is generally late.
Ambai	Only one-fifth satisfied. Poor teaching and the teacher is absent most of the time.
Kesaria	About half were satisfied. The appointment of a female teacher was seen as having improved teaching.

Source: Srivastava 1998.

outside the classroom. Teachers and peers often convey a distinct message of social inferiority to scheduled caste children. Overt discrimination has been exacerbated by the composition of the teaching corps. Most teachers are from non-scheduled castes and hence may not be sufficiently sensitive to cultural issues for scheduled caste students. Research in low-literacy districts in eight Indian states (World Bank 1997a, p. 138), found that schools with a high concentration of scheduled tribe students had fewer of the type of resources often associated with higher learning achievement: fewer pukka buildings (Madhya Pradesh, Orissa), less furniture and equipment (Kerala, Marahashtra, Orissa, Tamil Nadu), fewer instructional aids (Assam, Tamil Nadu), fewer teachers educated to grade 10 or above (Assam, Madhya Pradesh, Tamil Nadu), and fewer teachers with recent in-service training (Assam, Madhya Pradesh, Marahashtra, Orissa, Tamil Nadu).

The poor suffer doubly from poor quality. In addition to being in schools with superior services, children from better-off households benefit from their parents' inputs into the schooling process, such as making sure that the child attends school and does homework, and pushing school management and teachers to do a better job. Allocation of better-off household resources (whether in terms of money or time) to increase the quality of schooling will then have positive external effects, reaped by poor children in the same school. These positive externalities disappear, and impair further the already poor quality of schooling, when schools are concentrated in predominantly poor and socially disadvantaged villages.

The impact of this social or community-specific quality effect on demand for schooling by the poor is consistent with other findings from village studies in UP and Bihar and other states in India (Kozel et al. 1998, Drèze et al. 1996, World Bank 1997a). Empirical estimations of such community-specific effects show that both village and district averages of parents' education and wealth are important determinants of school attendance and achievements. The results show that children's school attendance depends not only on their parents' education level and income but also on the average level of education and income of other households in the village or the

district. In Himachal Pradesh, for example, demand for schooling, particularly for girls, increases due to the impact of the Total Literacy Campaign (TLC).

What are the implications for public policy?

If India is to meet its objective of sustaining high rates of economic growth with equity, then schooling must reach the economically and socially disadvantaged. Policy makers, who have often opted to expand the number of schools as a means of increasing enrollment of the poor, may need to reexamine that premise and its corollary that improvements in quality assist only the children of the rich, already enrolled and therefore the presumed principal beneficiaries of higher-quality education. Analyses are uncovering a different reality: the poor may not be in school *precisely because* of its low quality. The analysis carried out for this report clearly shows that states' success in reaching the poor and bringing them into the education system explains the differences in attainment across income groups within and across states. To include the children of the poor more fully in the educational system, India needs policies that can expand the quantity and quality of schooling and that work to eliminate the consequences in education of social exclusion based on income, gender, or caste. Box 2.2 summarizes the main recommendations for reform, discussed in greater details in the 1997 World Bank report on primary education. This report focuses on the potential for decentralization to improve the quality of education.

Public actions to raise the enrollment of the poor

Constitutionally, education is a concurrent responsibility of both central and state governments. State governments fund almost all recurrent expenditures for primary education and around 63 percent of the plan expenditures. The central government is responsible for developing education policy in cooperation with the states and also finances the rest of plan expenditures. In 1993 the central government, in close consultation with the states, intensified its efforts to increase enrollment, retention, and quality of primary education through the DPEP (Box 2.3), an innovative and initially well-financed reform program aimed at strengthening primary education, with a strong focus on quality to implement the recommendations of the 1986 National Policy on Education (NEP). Through the DPEP, the Government of India provides grants to states equivalent to 85 percent of the cost of approved investment, with the states providing the balance for programs targeted to districts with below-average female literacy rates. The NEP was updated in 1992, with sharper priorities given to girls and to improved quality in primary education under an integrated and decentralized approach to the development of primary education systems, so that districts gain greater capacity to plan and manage primary education. The remarkable accomplishments of the DPEP in increasing enrollment in lower primary education notwithstanding, about 33 million 6- to 10-year-olds are still not in school and three-quarters of them live in AP, Bihar, Madhya Pradesh, Orissa, Rajasthan, UP, and West Bengal.

The policy prescriptions for bringing these children into school are, however, less obvious because they depend on a strong political commitment to educate the children of the poor. To start, enforcement of the legislation for compulsory basic education is urgently required. There is no question that spending levels on education inputs (teachers, classrooms, textbooks, and instructional materials) need to increase. Box 2.2 provides estimates of the resource needs to put all children 6- to 14-year-olds in school.

Box 2.2: The basics of reform: specific challenges

To stay the course and increase the pace of improvement, the central, state, and local governments will need to focus clearly on the basics of school reform: what is required to get children into school, to keep them for the full primary cycle, and to enable them to learn. The specific challenges are many, but the following stand out as priorities.

Improving access and efficiency. With a basic system in place, attention should now turn to enrolling the 32 million primary-school-age children presently out of school and keeping those children in school for the full cycle. The key is to increase family demand for education and to improve school quality. Some reanalysis of the strategies in place to increase demand may be needed.

Enhancing learning achievement. Raising the very low levels of learning achievement in rural schools is essential if children are to gain basic skills. This will require sustained attention to improving the quality of key inputs and of school management, including community participation.

Reducing the gaps in enrollment, retention, and achievement. Targeted strategies for girls and for scheduled caste and scheduled tribe children—strategies based on research and carefully monitored—can help achieve these goals.

Improving teachers' performance. Improving the ability of teachers to function effectively in small rural schools with students of widely ranging ages is the central challenge in raising learning achievement. In-service training, stronger participation by community organizations and local governments, and more effective and efficient preservice education for teachers are all promising approaches, although none is easy to implement.

Improving the quality of textbooks and the efficiency of their production. Textbooks carry the curriculum and are the principal source of knowledge and instructional guidance for students and teachers alike. Having accomplished the massive task of providing textbooks to virtually all students, educational authorities now face the challenge of improving the quality of textbooks and the efficiency of their production.

Building managerial and institutional capacity. Giving local communities responsibility for primary education and recognizing the importance of good school management for school performance place management of change squarely on the reform agenda. Developing management systems and managers for this new kind of work is a formidable task.

Increasing financing for primary education. Based on reasonable assumptions regarding the cost of classrooms to be built, teachers' salaries, provision of books and other incentives, total requirements are projected at Rs. 195 billion in 2007 at 1993 prices. This includes improving schooling quality through rebuilding or rehabilitation of classrooms in need of major repairs, provision of drinking water and toilet facilities, and provision of instructional material and teacher training. Approximate estimation suggests that the required resources can be obtained if India grows by 5 percent in real terms and share of GDP spent on education increases. However, in an era of fiscal discipline, providing adequate resources for universal schooling will require both sustained political will and a better analytical understanding of the present—and possible—patterns of education finance.

Source: World Bank 1997a.

That said, the empirical findings in this report and those of other research in India (Filmer and Pritchett 1997, Drèze et al. 1996, World Bank 1997a) produce a consistent picture that *increasing resources will not be enough to improve enrollment and attainment of the poor*. Figures 2.2 and 2.3 illustrate this crucial point. Since the children of the better-off are in school independently of its quality, improvement in quality of schooling is crucial to attract poor children to school and retain them there. Because the opportunity costs are high for them and their families, poor children will not go to school if they perceive it as a waste of their time. The first pannel of Figure 2.2 shows that indiscriminate spending on elementary education alone will not increase the enrollment of the poor. This is supported by the findings of a huge literature which shows that while additional spending has the *potential*

to raise school quality, it will not necessarily do so. Similarly, the first pannel of Figure 2.3 shows no clear relationship between total state-level expenditure on elementary education and a reduction in the gap in enrollment of children from different economic groups.

In contrast, the second panels of Figures 2.2 and 2.3 show that expenditure (by both of parents and the government) on textbooks (a measure of quality of schooling) increases the probability of poor children enrolling, thus reducing the gaps in enrollment between the rich and the poor. States with higher levels of expenditures on textbooks have much lower gaps in the enrollment rates between the rich and poor. These empirical results are indicative. They do not literally mandate a single-minded focus on textbooks alone, but buttress instead three points about state-level educational policies. *First*, there is a need to spend

---

Box 2.3: District Primary Education Program (DPEP)

The Central Government, 14 state governments (AP, Assam, Bihar, Gujarat, Haryana, Himachal Pradesh, Karnataka, Kerala, Madhya Pradesh, Maharashtra, Orissa, Tamil Nadu, UP and West Bengal), and the World Bank have an intensive dialogue on primary education. This dialogue, which includes key Indian research institutions, partner agencies, and many parts of the civil society, is being supported by five IDA-financed projects (totaling over US$1 billion): Uttar Pradesh Basic Education Projects (UPBEP) I and II and DPEP I, II, and III.

These projects support replicable, sustainable, and cost-effective interventions aimed at (i) expanding access to lower primary school or its equivalent non-formal education for all children from socially disadvantaged groups (girls, scheduled castes and tribes, working children, children with mild to moderate learning disabilities, and other poor children who have limited access to educational opportunities); UPBEP also expands access to upper primary school for 11- to 13-year-olds; (ii) increasing retention and improving learning achievements through strengthened community participation, early childhood education, curriculum and textbook revision, in-service teacher training, targeted programs for women and girls, and strengthened school management; and (iii) strengthening the capacity of national, state, district, subdistrict and community institutions and organizations for the planning, management, and evaluation of primary education.

The UPBEP and DPEP now cover almost 150 low-literacy and socially disadvantaged districts in 14 Indian states with about 38 million children enrolled in primary schools. Another 36 districts in AP, UP and Rajasthan (to become the 15th DPEP state) with an additional enrollment of about 9 million children are in the pipeline. The second-generation DPEP interventions are part of statewide economic and fiscal reform programs (Andhra Pradesh, Rajasthan).

The emerging evidence from the projects' management information system and other preliminary research findings indicates that DPEP districts outperformed non-DPEP districts in enrollment (4 to 17 percentage points, with girls' enrollment accounting for over 51 percent of the total increase) and learning achievements over 1993-97. According to study by NIEPA (1997) on access and retention, enrollments increased by an average 8.5 percent (about 630,000 children) over 1995-96 for 39 of the 42 DPEP I districts. This was significantly higher than the average increase in primary school enrollment India-wide (2.5 percent). The index for gender equity is reported to be more than 95 for 18 out of 36 DPEP districts for which data are available.

Preliminary reports of learning assessment studies conducted in five DPEP I states suggest some improvement in learning skills in language and mathematics. Data to assess the DPEP's impact on increasing student retention and teacher attendance will soon be available. The increase in enrollment has also led to an increase in other educational inputs, such as new schools (about 4,700), classrooms (over 6,300), teachers, textbooks, teaching and learning materials, toilets, and drinking water facilities at the school sites.

more and spend better to achieve the goal of universal basic education. ***Second,*** while expanding access may bring the poor into schools, it may not retain them up to grade 5, let alone the grade 8, without significant improvement of the *quality* of basic education. ***Third,*** specific actions—among them the interventions under the DPEP and other initiatives such as the Lok Jumbish—intended to raise the quality of education for all children and targeted to poorer districts will improve the quality of schooling. Other interventions, such as Early Childhood Development programs, will help reduce the gender bias and improve learning achievement of the poor. *Focusing on those actions is a top priority*.

Improving quality of education needs fundamental reforms to change the incentives framework within which teachers, school officials, bureaucrats, and politicians operate. The accumulated experience under the DPEP and Lok Jumbish, and the experiences of states such as Kerala and Himachal Pradesh, should be analyzed to help provide the information necessary to underpin such deeper educational reforms, particularly in the seven states with the highest incidence of school dropouts or non-enrollment. Interesting findings from recent theoretical and empirical research (Filmer and Pritchett 1998) on educational production functions provide some guidance to reforms that are likely to improve outcomes. These include decentralization of control over the provision of schooling to the schools themselves, direct parental involvement, competition through school choice, and community involvement. Some of these reforms are already underway in many states in India. Madhya Pradesh, for example, is by far

Figure 2.2: Spending per student and enrollment

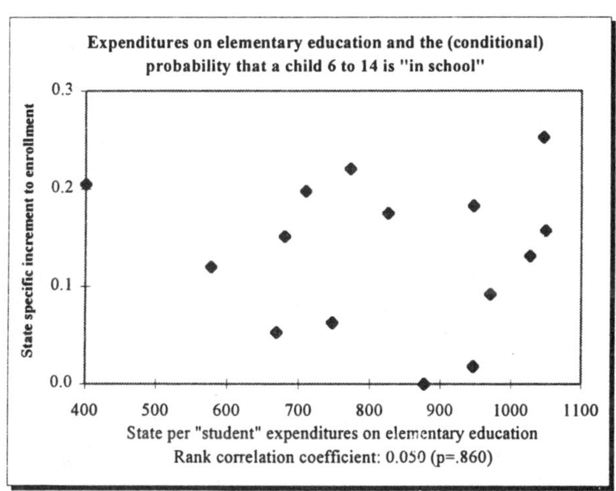

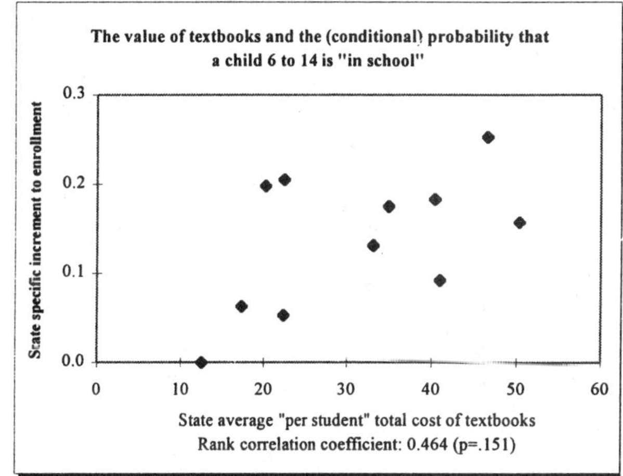

Figure 2.3: Spending per student and the gap in enrollment between the richest and poorest group

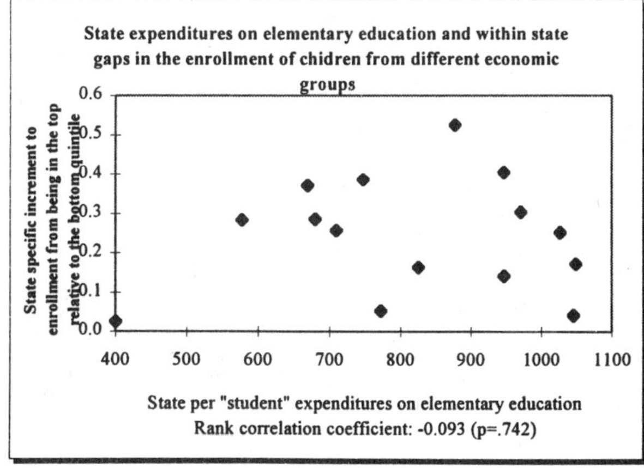

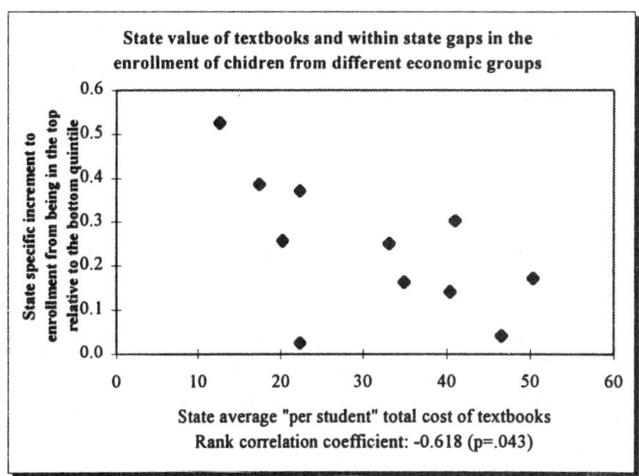

the most advanced in decentralizing school management to Panchayati Raj Institutions (PRIs) with a consequent increase in enrollment and retention among children of underprivileged groups (Box 2.4).

Can decentralization improve delivery of education services to the poor? Too early to tell? Following 1992 amendments to the constitution, India's states have only recently begun sorting out their new options for transferring control over primary, secondary, adult, non-formal, and vocational education and technical training to local-level (PRIs), few of which have management experience in the field. The process and the potential for bringing education closer to its users and beneficiaries has generated significant optimism but considerable caution. Decentralization is expected to increase accountability and efficiency, but there are fears that it could jeopardise equity. This section discusses each of these issues in turn.

The increased power of *voice,* through decentralization, as control of services is brought within "shouting distance" of users and expected to lead to improvements in cost-effectiveness through increased *accountability* and a ***better match between local preferences and conditions***. Internationally, one school of thought argues that decentralization can improve school performance only *if* it leads to school autonomy and only if it empowers users. There is a rich literature examining the relationship between the level and composition of educational spending and the output of the educational process by use of evidence based on cost-effectiveness methods, education production functions estimates, or direct evidence from differences in performance according to parental control within educational systems (see Filmer and Pritchett 1998 for a review). An important part of this literature maintains that school autonomy and direct parental influence—through school boards for example—are needed to improve school performance. Others argue that offering parents a choice of schools (private or public) through financial incentives improves efficiency because schools will be forced to improve quality or risk losing students and the associated revenue. An example from Himachal Pradesh illustrates how useful it can be when decision

---

Box 2.4: Decentralization of education management to PRIs: Madhya Pradesh's experience

The Panchayati Raj legislations of the states provide for standing committees at the district, block, and gram Panchayat level empowered to take decisions regarding education, including supervising and monitoring primary and secondary schools and education programs, mobilizing the community for enrollment and retention of children in schools, and building and repairing.

The most far-reaching experience of devolution of primary schooling management to PRIs seems to be in Madhya Pradesh. Enrollments and retention among children of under privileged groups has increased, a result of an increased demand for primary schooling through the TLC. This demand was met in part through greater supply of schools and teachers under the DPEP, which is currently operational in 33 districts. Village education committees were made responsible for the construction and management of new primary schools. After the 73rd Amendment, gram panchayats were given the powers to recruit school teachers locally (called shiksha karmis) on a contractual basis and supervise them. These teachers are currently being recruited at the block level on the recommendation of the gram panchayats.

Since January 1997 the state has launched an innovative Education Guarantee Scheme (EGS). Under the scheme, any village unserved by a primary school within one k.m. and with more than 25 children (in tribal areas, or 40 children in non-tribal) out of school can demand assistance to set up a school, with the community providing the space. For its part, the state undertakes to provide within 90 days complementary teaching inputs and a salary to a locally appointed contractual teacher (Guruji). Over the first months of its existence, more than 15,000 EGS schools have been set up. In the 2,300 EGS schools for which enrollment figures are available, of the nearly 88,000 students enrolled around 47 percent were girls. The EGS has paved the way to a demand-driven educational expansion in Madhya Pradesh. The school management committees have been gradually decentralized and operate at the village level. The government has recently transferred assets of primary and secondary schools, as well as personnel, to the PRIs. This may further increase the involvement of communities as stakeholders. On the whole, the impact of decentralization, which has been backed by vigorous campaigns, appears to be quite positive in Madhya Pradesh. The demand-driven expansion of schooling in remote areas through the EGS confirms the importance of community involvement in increasing the enrollment of the poor.

Source: R. Srivastava 1998.

makers are within shouting distance, whether voice takes formal channels or not. In Khalimi, a suburb of Shimla, the state capital, the community organized a rally of 400 persons who were outraged by non-performing teachers, all selected by wrongful criteria and not teaching. They marched to the state's chief minister to demand the teachers' removal, and eventually all were transferred. There are numerous other examples across India. Through decentralization, political, bureaucratic, and other channels for voice are made less costly and possibly more efficient. If a problem is school specific, then it is easier to push for action if an entity is near and responsible for one or a few schools rather than far and responsible for thousands.

Closer proximity, better information, and local knowledge can lead to increased accountability. While lower levels of institutional capacity may be weak and local power structures biased, local governments—such as the gram panchayats—may nonetheless have other factors that compensate for these weaknesses. Proximity gives them an advantage in both monitoring and reacting faster and directly. Incentives are the other powerful instrument at their disposal. A community may be better placed to really watch and react appropriately. As potential beneficiary of the assets to be created (the children's human capital, in this case), the family is genuinely interested in quality and efficiency, while for a bureaucrat, such an interest has to be created by institutional design. Few doubt that parents have a cost advantage in monitoring problems such as teacher absenteeism, and that the critical issue is whether they can be given adequate powers to react.

This requires transparency and easy access to information, which may be lacking if there are large initial inequalities and if the potential clients are marginalized by poverty and illiteracy. Accountability of local officials may pose a challenge when local governments are not confined to spending what they have collected from their constituencies. Most states have allowed PRIs little ability or authority to mobilize resources. Own revenues (from taxes and fees) form a significant resource base in only a few states, such as Kerala, Gujarat, and Maharashtra. When resources (whether in the form of staff or money) come from afar, discipline from citizens who check that they get

their benefits presupposes that they are informed of the resources availability and know who is in control. In some states, such as West Bengal, a combination of policy initiatives and political mobilization have put pressure on elected leadership to share information and increased demand for such information. In other states, privileged information, helped by complex administrative rules, has been nurtured and exploited by officials as a major source of corruption. Attempts to address this problem are recent government orders and legislation on "freedom of information" in states such as Madhya Pradesh, Rajasthan, and UP. Mandatory holding of general meetings (gram sabhas) and social audits and posting of information regarding receipts and expenditures are being tried out with various degrees of success. These measures, combined with the strong independent journalism in India, social mobilization, political competition, and controls and performance audits from higher-level governments, hold the promise of improving the effectiveness of "people as monitors" and reducing leakages and corruption.

Another important ingredient is whether local institutions (PRIs or school committees, for instance) obtain the necessary powers to impose accountability. Without such powers, the community cannot hold PRIs accountable for school performance, and decentralization will therefore not make a difference. In India today, to take one example, transfer of staff to undesirable areas is the only available instrument to penalize chronic non-performers, and even this recourse may be blocked by political intervention. State line ministry officials as well as PRI representatives argued—quite fairly—that the issue of staff performance is linked to the broader problem of civil service performance, which is far beyond their powers and responsibilities. However, some states have already started to experiment with contractual staff in teaching (Himachal Pradesh, Rajasthan) and PRI-devolved teacher hiring (Madhya Pradesh) as ways of increasing their ability to manage staff accountability and improve school performance.

Another benefit of decentralization is the allocative efficiency gains local governments are thought to bring through matching of program design to local conditions and preferences. The following illustrates that local decision making had to be relied upon to solve a local problem. In an effort to enroll more girls in primary schools in Rajasthan, the Lok Jumbish project chose an approach based on gender-based mobilization, school mapping, and microplanning. School mapping is based on local conditions, while microplanning is an interactive process involving the local community in finding solutions to the community's problems. In a remote Muslim community with less than 10 percent girl enrollment, it took about two years to build confidence and design solutions for enrolling girls in school. For acceptance, it proved important to change hours so that school attendance would not conflict with religious teaching in the mosque. Also the community was more interested teaching in Urdu than in Hindi, and now the schools are teaching both. Over a four period, enrollments increased to 65 percent, according to Lok Jumbish's statistics (1998). This is not short of remarkable if it can be sustained, and a great gift to other areas if it can be replicated. In Himachal Pradesh, state authorities are increasingly relying on PRIs to help increase demand from the remote areas for education. One of the great benefits of decentralization is that it offers a broad field for innovation and experimentation that might lead to successful models which will be replicated and sustained.

Finally, the chief fear—that decentralization could perpetuate, and quite possibly increase, regional disparities in school quality and social and economic inequities in access to good schooling if funding levels for education drop—may not materialize if the central and state governments retain responsibility for redistributive goals. Under a decentralized system of provision and funding at the district or village level, the poor may be almost as badly served as if they had to fend for themselves (Table 2.6). So, even if PRIs are given complete autonomy over school management, it is important that that both central and state governments continue to fund primary education.

Equity considerations should not, however, create adverse incentives for performance. In a system seeking in part to support the poor, there is always the danger that incentives are created—either for lower-level governments or for individuals—either to appear poor or not to perform well enough to grow. For example, states such as Kerala and Himachal Pradesh are concerned that if they continue to do well, they will receive less funds from the center. Reducing the risk of penalizing the good performers and rewarding the poor performers on equity considerations requires improving the design of current intergovernmental transfers. The latter have built-in negative incentive effects which have discouraged state fiscal discipline and reduced allocative efficiency. In this context it is unfortunate that the current process of decentralization through PRIs is taking place without a corresponding reform of the center-state transfer mechanisms.

Link between health, nutrition and schooling. In addition to raising school quality, there are specific actions that can increase the demand for schooling by raising its benefits, reducing its costs, or otherwise lowering the barriers to participation of the children of the poor in education. There is substantial evidence that healthy and well-nourished children use educational inputs more productively. Children who experience early growth failure as a result of

Table 2.6: Change in service quality for lowest 40 percent of households with decentralization				
	Nationally-funded (base case)	State-funded	District-funded	Village-funded	Household-funded (comparison)
AP	100	0	-9	-25	-41
Bihar	100	-17	-31	-43	-53
Kerala	100	+9	+4	-2	-17
Rajasthan	100	0	-13	-28	-41
Tamil Nadu	100	+3	-9	-20	-36
UP	100	-6	-25	-31	-46

Note: The quality indicator represents the uniform service quality (measured by funding) that could be supported by the mean wealth of each jurisdiction, setting All India's to 100. So under national provision, India's bottom 40 percent of households will have a service quality of 100. The household comparison (last column) is the cutoff wealth level for the poorest 40 percent of households in the state sample. Assuming that quality is proportional to expenditure is optimistic, since wealthier jurisdictions also will have higher quantity and quality of other inputs such as parents' time.
Source: Eskeland 1998.

malnutrition or infection are more likely to delay enrollment. Undernutrition is also found to have a greater impact on poor children's cognitive and behavioral development than on the development of children who are not poor (Martorell 1997). Protein-energy malnutrition, temporary hunger, and micronutrient deprivation all adversely affect learning achievement. Moreover, persistent illnesses that foster repeated absence from school impair learning (Lockheed and Verspoor, 1991).

For a child the early years are critical. By investing in programs that target nutrition, health care, and access to safe water for children zero to eight years of age, these programs follow children from preschool to early primary school years and help them form a sound foundation for continued growth and development. Simulations using a hypothetical cohort of 100 children from a low-income country with social indicators similar to those of India show that more than half of the 100 children will never have a chance to reach their full potential. Some will die, although most will survive. Of those who survive, many will become subsistence farmers, inhabitants of shanty towns, illiterate and ill-prepared for modern, industrial, competitive economies (van der Gaag 1996).

Sound public policies need to be designed for the children who survive to protect them from malnutrition and disease and to provide the health care, preschool and primary education, and related areas (for example, water and sanitation) that will enable them to reach their full potential. Without appropriate interventions, the vicious circle of poverty will capture them and the next generation and generations thereafter. India has a plethora of nutrition and child development programs (see Chapter 4), but they have not been as effective as hoped in raising the nutritional status of poor children (World Bank 1997b). Early evidence indicates that the midday meals program seems to be having a positive impact on school attendance, at least, but most observers doubt that it has had an impact on nutritional status of children. Chapter 3 of this report provides some recommendations on maximizing the benefits to the poor from public spending on health, to improve their health status. The findings of the forthcoming study on reducing the incidence of malnutrition among poor children should help in the design of coherent and effective public policies for the development of India's

poor children. Of particular importance are the needed reforms to transform the current Integrated Child Development Services (ICDS) into a more effective program for early child development (Chapter 4).

Gender-specific actions. Although a range of strategies has been proposed in rural low-literacy districts to reduce the gender gap in enrollment and dropout rates, few have been comprehensively tested. Some aim at lowering the opportunity cost to parents of educating their girls by offering direct incentives such as grants, vouchers, or direct provision of fees, books, food, uniforms, and transport. Others target the supply side: increasing the number of schools for girls, appointing more female teachers, opening NFE centers, constructing toilets for girls. A rigorous evaluation of the impacts of these programs is needed to find out which ones are working. The sparse available evidence shows that—like the anti-poverty programs—not all the intended beneficiaries are benefiting from the cash-based incentives. Here again there is an urgent need to carefully examine the results achieved under the Lok Jumbish and DPEP projects to see what works and what could be replicated to raise girls enrollments and learning achievements.

That said, results from effective ECD programs suggest that their benefits could help reduce the gender gap in India. ECD programs enable older siblings, particularly sisters, to attend school by releasing them from the responsibility of providing daily childcare for their younger brothers and sisters. Parents' involvement in ECD activities also helps, because parents acquire knowledge that also goes to their daughters about good nutrition, health risks and health behaviors, learning and cognition, parent-child interactions, family relationships, and other related subjects in early childcare and development. This acquired knowledge and awareness will benefit their daughters, reducing the likelihood of parental discrimination against their daughters in food intake, health care, and education. These benefits underscore the urgent need to reform the ICDS into an effective program for early child development activities.

Education pays significant dividends in reducing poverty. Good education pays high returns in the contributions to economic growth a more skilled, more aware, more responsive work force can make to accelerate a nation's development. Educating the poor, women, and the disadvantaged is as good an investment as any India can make. India faces many educational challenges and particularly those of narrowing or closing the gaps between rich and poor, boys and girls, privileged groups and undercastes. All the evidence—including the experience of different Indian states and other non-governmental initiatives— points to the possibility of meeting those challenges successfully; the need for substantial and steady funding of education, whether from central or other resources; and the value of quality learning for the poor.

CHAPTER 3: POVERTY, HEALTH STATUS, AND HEALTH POLICY TO REDUCE POVERTY

Of the assets needed to grow out of poverty, good health ranks as high as education. *No country can secure sustainable economic growth or poverty reduction without a healthy, well-nourished, and educated population.* Yet more than a third of India's population is poor, malnourished, illiterate, and in bad health. While India has succeeded over the last four decades in doubling life expectancy and reducing infant mortality, its death rate for infants under five remains one of the highest in the world. Communicable diseases and prenatal and maternal mortality, which account for 12.5 percent of the annual deaths of rural women aged 15 to 45, cause about 470 deaths per 100,000 population in India—a rate four times that of China and 2.5 times that of the world as a whole. Tuberculosis (TB) alone kills 500,000 people a year. Half of all children under five are malnourished and, because their mothers often are as well, one-third of all newborn babies are underweight. And fewer than half the children from poor households are in school, reducing their prospects for escaping the poverty that plagued their parents' lives.

For a variety of reasons poor individuals are unable to make sufficient investments in themselves or their children, which justifies a role for government's intervention in promoting equity. Public spending is a potentially powerful instrument for fighting poverty if it actually reaches the poor by helping them gain better access to public goods and services. In general public subsidies will benefit the poor most when the items subsidized are used disproportionately by the poor relative to the non-poor (Box 4.1, Annex 3.2). If it is possible to identify the poor and deliver these services exclusively to them, then the provision of any medical care (or anything else, for that matter, even cash transfers) would do equally well and would serve as a perfectly good redistributive device. For cases where poor individuals cannot be identified perfectly, indirect targeting methods are required. In health the distributional effect of services can be assessed through geographic targeting, i.e., providing services in areas where the poor are in disproportionate numbers, or it can be assessed by type of provider, if people choose different venues for treatment according to their income, or by type of disease. This chapter examines the relative burden of disease of the poor and its determinants, as well as the extent to which the poor have benefited from public spending on certain health services.

Based on the findings of this benefit incidence analysis, the chapter discusses options for providing or financing those services that are most likely to have a greater impact on the health status of poor households and their children. While of critical importance to the poor, nutrition and reproductive health policies are not discussed here because they are the subject of more in-depth treatment in other studies.

In addition to other sources of information, the chapter uses the 1992-93 NFHS data set, which contains nearly identical household surveys done in each of the major states, with smaller states combined regionally. The NFHS data contain information on approximately 88,000 households, 500,000 individuals, and 34,000 births in the two years preceding the survey. Not only is the sample very large, it also includes three types of data that are hard to find in the same household survey: household living conditions, the prevalence of different disease conditions, and the use of public health facilities. Because the NFHS data did not contain questions about income or consumption (which are used to measure poverty), it has been widely assumed that such data are not suitable for the assessment of differences in health status across income groups. However, since the surveys do ask questions about ownership of a wide variety of consumer durables and other household assets, it was possible to construct an index of wealth or socio-economic status against which health status and service use can be measured (see Annex 2 for the construction of such an index). This is an important contribution as recent burden of disease assessments have not distinguished between the problems of the poor and those of the rich. A second drawback of the survey is that a full description of the burden of disease on the poor is not possible since the survey's coverage of various disease conditions is limited. However, this is not an important limitation when discussing the general types of illnesses that affect the poor most, which should therefore form the focus of poverty reduction strategies.

The research carried out for this report found that the poor face a disproportionately higher risk than the rich of falling sick, particularly from infectious diseases. They are more likely to lose their children before they reach the age of two. Poor members of scheduled castes run even higher risks of premature death. And because the poor are less likely to be educated and must often use shared sources of water and surface water (lakes, streams, ponds) without adequate sanitation facilities, they are dangerously exposed to illness and premature death. The study further finds that the public sector is failing to deliver the promised care to reduce India's high infant mortality. These issues are discussed in turn in the following sections.

Health status of the poor

It should come as no surprise that poor people are in worse health than others. Bad health and premature death are, arguably, the most tragic manifestations of poverty. Figures 3.1-3.3 show the dependence of several health indicators by quintiles of wealth. These are the under-two child mortality rate (Figure 3.1), and whether a household member is currently suffering from TB, leprosy, blindness, or limb impairment or has had malaria in the past month of the survey (Figure 3.2). Figure 3.3 shows the probability of a child having had diarrhea, "fever with rapid breathing," or symptoms of acute respiratory infection (ARI), in the two weeks preceding the survey. The ratios of the occurrence of these diseases between the poorest and richest quintiles are summarized in Table 3.1, showing, for example, that a member of a poor household is over four times more likely to contract TB and over three

times more likely to get malaria than a member of a rich household. Even this limited data set shows that the poor suffer disproportionately more from communicable and vector (pest) borne diseases, which is also borne out by other analyses. TB, malaria, and leprosy, as well as the mortality rate of children under two (which is dominated by diarrhea and respiratory ailments), are all examples of such diseases. This pattern of greater correlation between income and communicable diseases has been noted in other countries (Murray et al., 1992).

The findings of this study further confirm earlier studies' results that disparities in health status between rich and poor in India are much more important for communicable than non-communicable diseases (Annex 3.1, Tables 4-9 show the results of the

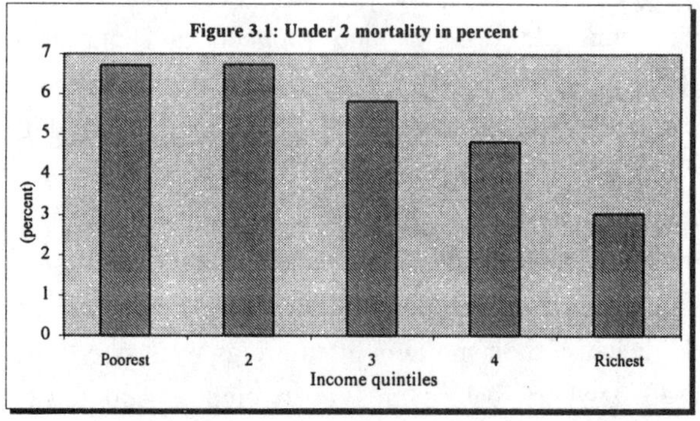

Figure 3.1: Under 2 mortality in percent

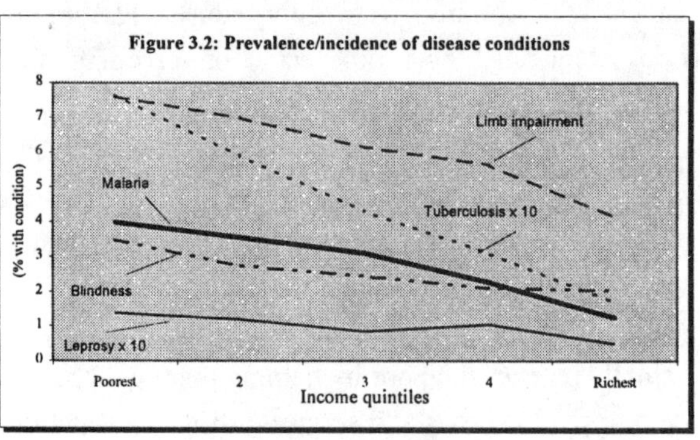

Figure 3.2: Prevalence/incidence of disease conditions

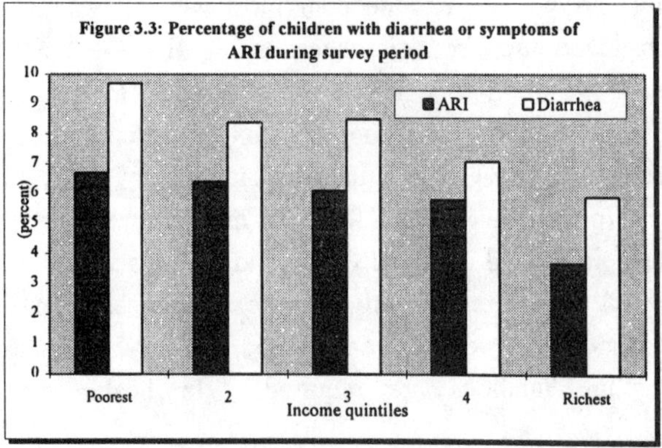

Figure 3.3: Percentage of children with diarrhea or symptoms of ARI during survey period

econometric analyses for the other disease conditions as presented in Figures 3.1-3.2). Non-communicable diseases are not as closely linked to poverty as the communicable diseases.

Determinants of health status of the poor

What determines good health and illness? Several factors influence the variability in health status across income groups. These are (i) factors not directly related to policy—income, occupation, personal characteristics, and state of residence; (ii) factors related to policies outside the health sector—education levels, access to electricity or good roads; (iii) factors partly related to health policy but in the nature of public goods or with important external effects, such as water, sanitation, and vaccinations; and (iv) factors related to clinical care, such as access to a Primary Health Center (PHC), subcenter, hospitals, and other publicly provided medical services.

Variables independent of health policy influence mortality rates among children. In particular the study finds, controlling for the whole range of variables that (i) children of scheduled castes and of very young mothers are more likely to die before their second birthday; (ii) somewhat surprisingly, this effect is not found among children of scheduled tribes; and (iii) there are no clear independent effects on child survival from state policies not already accounted for by the state's level of income, education, and public infrastructure (Annex 3.1, Tables 1-3).

The role of underage mothers in complicating pregnancy and harming children's chances of survival is well documented in the literature. The surprising finding about the children of tribal people merits further investigation. It is possible that because tribal people live separately from others, if there is discrimination against them, it will be seen by the lack of roads, electricity, etc. which are already captured in the variables included in the regressions. Scheduled castes, on the other hand, being interspersed in communities, may be subject to discrimination not detected by the included variables. Why this should be true, independently of income and the other observable determinants listed above, is worthy of further analysis. What makes members of scheduled castes more prone to losing their children? Are they less able to take

Table 3.1: Prevalence of disease	
Condition	**Ratio poor to rich**
Tuberculosis	4.5
Malaria	3.2
Leprosy	2.8
Mortality (under 2)	2.2
Limb impairment	1.8
Blindness	1.7

advantage of even physically accessible public services? Do informal networks carry less health-related information to them? Or are more subtle aspects of social exclusion—going beyond wealth and poverty—at work and at fault?

Public policies outside the health sector have direct implications for health. Female education, if taken as a whole, and higher education levels in particular have their usual importance in protecting children. Similarly the study finds that in those areas where there is electricity, child mortality is reduced. Establishing the reasons for this may require further investigation. Electricity could be having an impact through its effect on safer food handling through refrigeration. It could also be capturing the effect of some omitted variables.

Turning to policies more directly related to health, immunizations save young lives, but many poor rural children go unvaccinated. Among the factors determining an Indian one-year-old's chances of reaching the age of five, no single element matters as much as vaccination, the study finds. Exactly why immunization should have such a strong effect, when the number of deaths from vaccine-preventable causes is not sufficient to explain much variation, is not clear. More importantly, because both income and education were controlled for, this strong effect of vaccination indicates that either there are more subtle determinants of demand or there is a distinct role for promotion from the supply side. Getting one's child vaccinated signals a particular parental interest in or sensitivity to health matters. Parents who vaccinate their children are perhaps more likely to be aware of the importance of good hygiene, safe food handling, and good nutrition. These are personal characteristics not properly accounted for in the econometric analysis, and more research is clearly warranted. In the meantime, there is sufficient evidence from India and elsewhere in the world that continuing the active promotion of free immunizations is important.

Water, privately accessible, is an important determinant of child survival, too. Access to sanitation and, especially, private access to water, are important for the survival of children under two in both urban and rural areas. The study further finds that when this effect is combined with differences in access to water and sanitation facilities across the income groups, it explains a substantial part of differences in mortality rates of poor children compared with those of the rich. Yet the poor are especially deprived of such life-saving access. Figures 3.4(a)-3.4(h) show the distribution of water, sanitation, and education across income categories and show, not surprisingly, that the healthier and wealthier have far better access to piped and other exclusive sources of water than the poor. The latter, reflecting the powerful role income plays in determining access to different sources of water and types of sanitation, rely heavily on shared sources and surface water (lakes, streams, ponds). That access, in turn, is a major determinant of vulnerability to or protection against many kinds of illness and disease.

But access to public health facilities is not among the determinants of child survival. Consistent with previous studies (Jain, 1988, Srinivasan 1988) which control for income and education, this study does not find any correlation between the availability of subcenters and PHCs and child survival—among either the poor or the non-poor.

One might think, given the strong results on vaccines, that the PHCs may be important as a vehicle for vaccination delivery. This makes sense but is not borne out by the data. Further, the study finds, there is no correlation between having a public facility in the village and being immunized when controlling for income and education. This is a plausible finding, since the government organizes an extensive annual drive for vaccinations using schools, ICDS centers, and other facilities.

The lack of impact shown in this analysis raises important issues. Both subcenters and PHCs should have had an effect on child survival at least in the way they have been set up. Subcenters are designed to provide vaccinations, family planning, are basic preventive and curative care, while PHCs treat children with ARI (Figure 3.5) and diarrhea and provide other

medical services which should have an impact on children. This means that either (a) the services are not oriented toward the type of care needed or located in areas where the poor cannot access them, (b) services are not functioning as they should, or (c) the large private sector (including unlicensed practitioner) is substituting for the public sector, especially for relatively inexpensive care.

Figure 3.6 shows that the presence of a PHC facility in the village is strongly related to income per se, while the presence of a subcenter is not. If for some reason those with better health (and health is related to wealth) end up with PHC facilities while those with worse health end up with subcenters, this would explain the absence of any direct effect of facilities on health outcomes. Subcenters might actually delay getting appropriate treatment. Furthermore, the land on which PHCs are built in poor villages is usually donated by rich landlords and situated far from the village. This may explain why the poor would not use them, if the opportunity cost is high relative to using a more easily accessible private doctor, particularly for relatively inexpensive treatment. In addition, having a building is not the same as having medical care. The difficulties in properly staffing, managing, and provisioning such facilities are myriad and well known (World Bank 1995b, 1997d) and borne out by evidence from village studies (Box 3.1).

Although this finding is limited to analysis of facility use in rural areas from the 1992-93 NFHS, it does suggest that India is not getting the returns it should from its spending on public health and, more importantly, that the poor are not benefiting from much of that spending. These results are consistent with the findings from the rich literature documenting the poor performance of India's publicly run health systems (World Bank 1997d).

However, the full benefits to the poor of publicly provided care may not be reflected merely in child survival, since the latter is only one of many possible indicators of health status. Further analysis is needed to assess the impact of public spending on health in other respects.

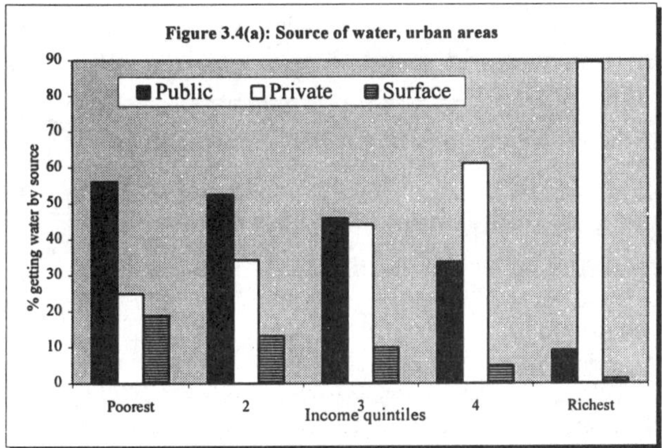

Figure 3.4(a): Source of water, urban areas

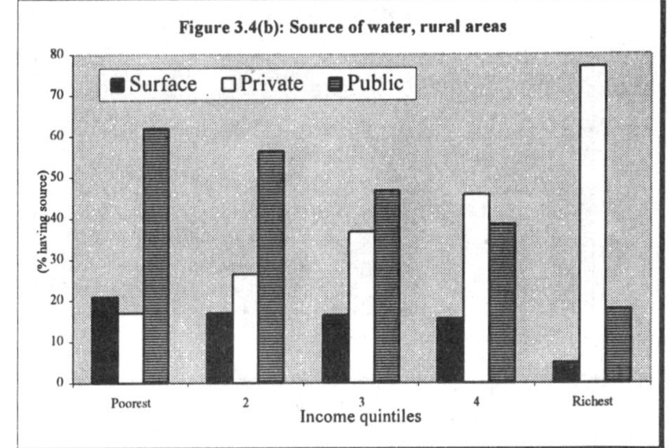

Figure 3.4(b): Source of water, rural areas

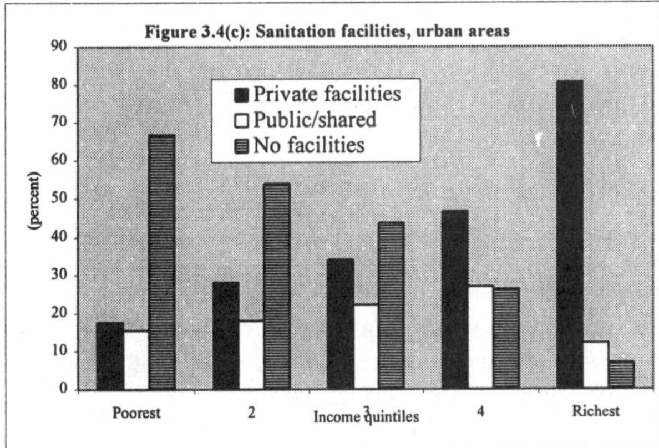

Figure 3.4(c): Sanitation facilities, urban areas

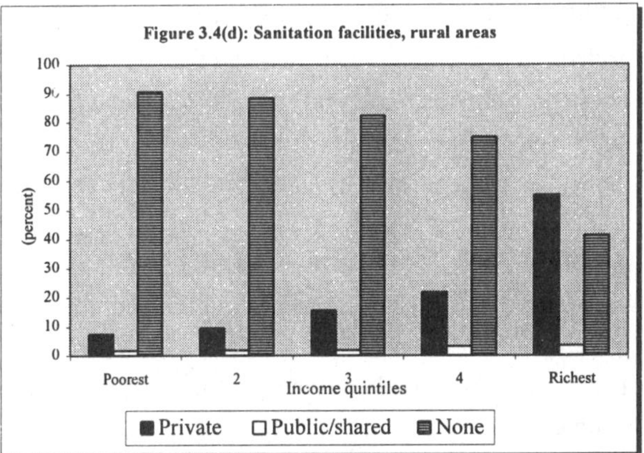

Figure 3.4(d): Sanitation facilities, rural areas

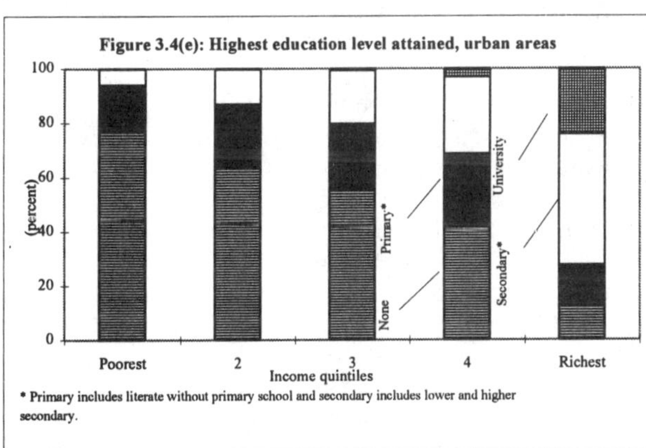

Figure 3.4(e): Highest education level attained, urban areas

* Primary includes literate without primary school and secondary includes lower and higher secondary.

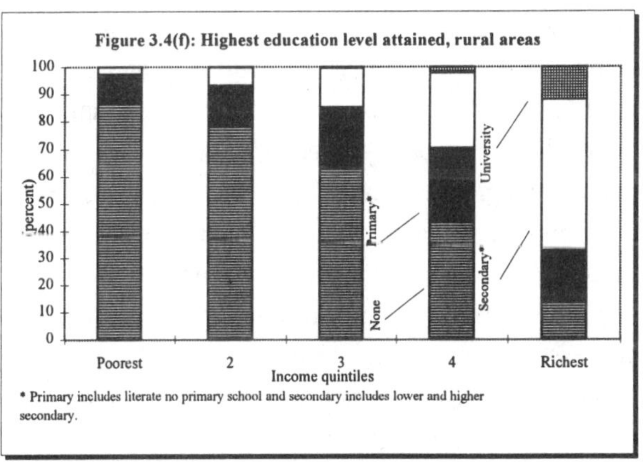

Figure 3.4(f): Highest education level attained, rural areas

* Primary includes literate no primary school and secondary includes lower and higher secondary.

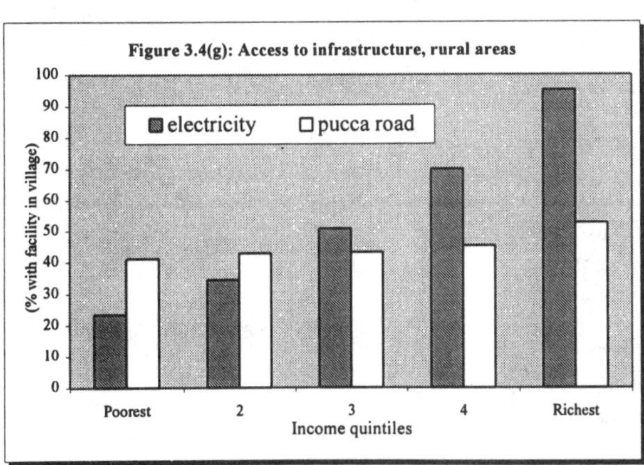

Figure 3.4(g): Access to infrastructure, rural areas

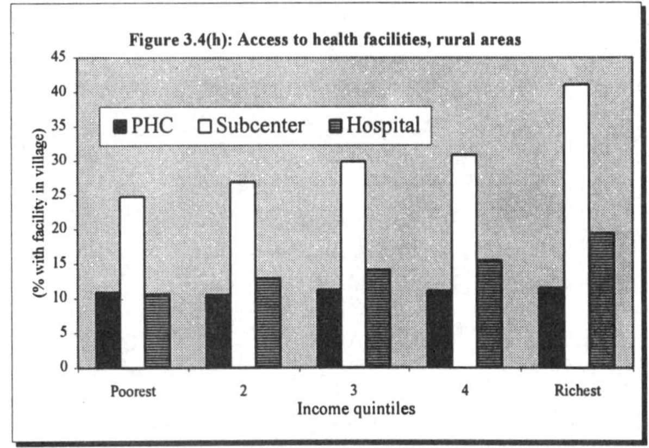

Figure 3.4(h): Access to health facilities, rural areas

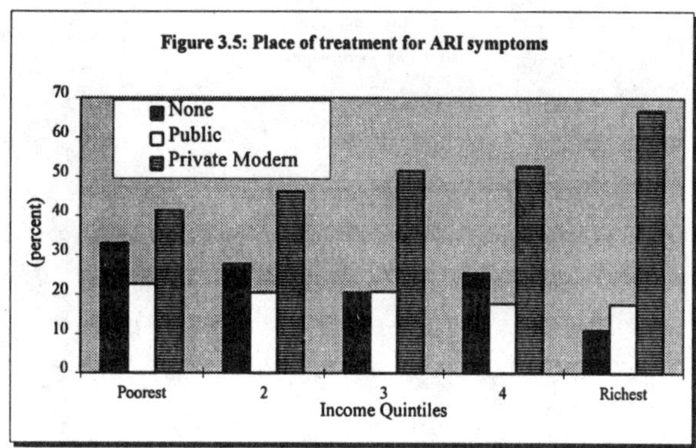

Figure 3.5: Place of treatment for ARI symptoms

In addition, because the use of public health facilities is quite equitably distributed, the quality of service provision determines demand for such services and hence the distributional impact of spending on such services. Figure 3.4(h) shows that while there is a slightly higher probability that better-off people in rural areas will have public medical facilities, the effect is quite small. At least in terms of physical availability, the distribution of public facilities is equitable. This brings to the forefront the importance of demand and supply issues in the health sector. While capital investments and the supply of inputs are necessary to increase access, they are not sufficient to improve outcomes. Demand is also an important factor, because goods must be consumed and services used to be effective, particularly when the latter are targeted to the poor. People's perceptions about quality and effectiveness of care, the attitude of health care providers, and the availability of essential consumables such as drugs have a dramatic impact on service utilization and health outcomes And carelessness in program management and execution, such as a momentary break in a vaccination cold-chain or inappropriate judgment on when to refer

complicated cases, can make entire programs ineffective (World Bank 1997e).

Box 3.1: Use of a public health facility
Evidence from village studies in UP and Bihar

In talks with villagers, interviewers seeking to understand how health services are used asked about the household's most recent serious illness or health crisis and about the deaths of any children and the actions taken during the preceding crisis. In addition villagers spontaneously raised health and disability issues during discussions of downward mobility in the Wealth Ranking Exercise.

From those conversations, *health problems emerged as one of the most common causes of persistent poverty*. In the Wealth Ranking Exercise, nearly every group mentioned disability of the breadwinner or the expense of treating long-term illnesses of various family members as factors which impoverished formerly self-sufficient middle-income households. In the worst cases, illness or disability led to debt bondage and the loss of economic autonomy. While the loss of wages of the economically productive members of the household is the greatest health threat to a household's well-being, even treatment costs for a non-earner can lead to the loss of assets. For this reason parents may find it is necessary to forgo treatment of a chronically ill child if they are to provide adequately for the rest of the household.

Strikingly, nearly all the informants said they do not use the government PHCs or subcenters, in some cases because no center is near and transport costs over poorly constructed and infrequently maintained link roads are too high when outcomes are so uncertain. Since medical staff assigned to PHC facilities are usually absent, even during the limited hours that are posted, the villagers reported, a trip to the center often translates into a waste of scarce money. In one area it was said that PHC operations near population centers and roads are better staffed and supervised, but medical personnel seldom visit the remote rural areas they are responsible for serving. Quality of care was not mentioned as an issue, but if care is generally unavailable, its quality is hardly relevant.

Even when medical staff members are on site, PHCs get little traffic because they do not have medicines on hand. Instead they distribute only prescriptions. Poor patients must visit the market and incur a second transport expense. Upper-income villagers, it was said, use either a private clinic or an urban government hospital. But even the latter, where—unlike most PHCs—qualified professionals are on hand, may run out of drugs and supplies.

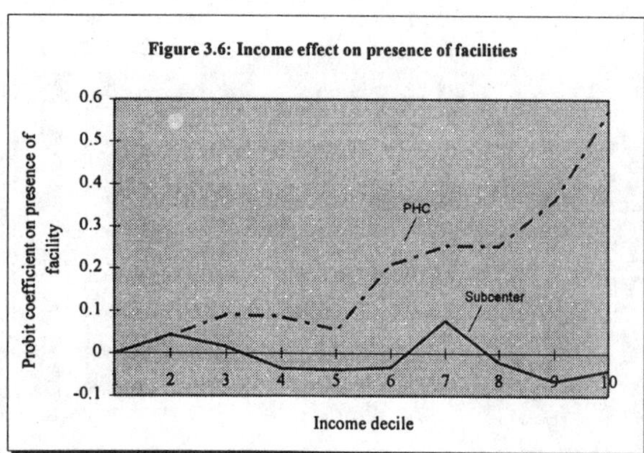

Figure 3.6: Income effect on presence of facilities

The lack of correlation between public health facilities and child survival could also be due to the difficulty of measuring impact in the absence of carefully collected information on health outcomes before and after service provision. This is consistent with recent World Bank evaluations of investment projects in health, nutrition, and population which concluded that it was difficult to attribute improvements in health status, nutrition, and fertility that have occurred during the past 20 years directly to such spending.

In sum, while it is not possible to come to any final conclusion about the effect of public health facilities on child survival, the evidence from this analysis, although partial, is not encouraging. Much more research is needed, for example, to understand fully how much of the lack of correlation is due to low quality of service provided, how much is due to interaction of demand for public and private services, and how much is mere statistical artifact. This should constitute a priority research area because the policy implications differ depending on whether the main reason is poor quality, the availability of an easily accessible and large private sector, or both.

What are the implications for health policy?

A number of policy implications can be derived from the NFHS. *First*, combating communicable diseases and expanding traditional public health interventions of guaranteeing safe water and sanitation, as well as disseminating information to the public on basic hygiene and the value of preventive care, would deliver the highest gains from public health spending, particularly for the poor. The application of targeting principles would argue for allocating public spending on the basis of relative burden of disease rather than its absolute burden. Attacking a problem which imposes a large burden on both the poor and non-poor alike is not as good a vehicle for achieving redistributive goals as one that imposes a small burden on the poor but a much smaller burden on the non-poor. Therefore, to the extent that public expenditures on health are meant to serve the poor disproportionately, it makes sense in India today to allocate public spending in favor of

dealing with communicable diseases. Non-communicable diseases such as cancers and heart disease are growing among the poor and will account for a larger share of total deaths or other measures of ill health than will infectious diseases. However, other things being equal, reallocating public spending from diseases with a higher poor to non-poor ratio of victims to a lower one will be regressive (Box 3.2). Interventions addressing non-communicable diseases are, in general, less well targeted to the poor than are those for communicable diseases.

A standard approach to setting priorities for public expenditures is to compare the degree of improvement over market allocations that different types of public spending will have. Traditional public health policies rank high in this regard as well as in their relative impact on rich and poor. It is not common to find policies in which there is such strong complementarity of equity and efficiency goals, and it is important not to let this opportunity go unexploited.

TB control is a good example. It attacks a disease with very clear external effects where every person effectively cured represents, on average, another saved from infection (Murray, Styblo, and Rovillon 1993). The cure, however, is long and costly relative to average Indian income levels, let alone those of the poor, and for well-established economic reasons, there is virtually no private insurance market in rural and (for most people) urban areas to cushion the expense. But if drug therapy is discontinued prematurely because symptoms have disappeared, not only does the disease reappear in patients, there is also an increased risk of contributing to the development of drug resistance. This is a clear and serious externality where individual action can substantially increase the cost to others. *On grounds of attacking severe externalities as well as the consequences of missing markets, TB control is a high-priority activity.* The distributional impact in favor of the poor is also very beneficial. Similarly, for diseases for which transmission is decreased by the number of children immunized, an immunization program will confer an external benefit in addition to the benefit gained by the immunized child.

<table>
<tr><td>

Box 3.2: Illustration of the importance of the relative burden of disease

Assume the government can prevent either of two diseases of comparable severity Also assume the government cannot distinguish between people who benefit from either program on the basis of their income, so that everyone who would have gotten the same disease has the same chance of benefiting from the prevention program. Cases attributable to these diseases per 1,000 population are as follows:

	Disease A	Disease B
Poor	7	21
Rich	1	14

Note that disease B affects more poor people than does disease A and disease B affects more poor people than it does rich people.

If the health authorities want to use their public spending to help the poor to the greatest extent possible, how should they allocate it between the different diseases? When public funds are spent on preventing disease B (the one with the greater burden on the poor), 60 percent of the beneficiaries would be poor since 21/(21+14)=0.6. When funds are spent on preventing disease A, however, 87.5 percent [(7/(7+1)=0.875] of the beneficiaries are poor. Therefore, even though the poor suffer more from disease B than A and also suffer from disease B more than do the rich, concentrating public spending on preventing disease A is a more progressive way of spending public money.

</td></tr>
</table>

The *second* area with highest returns for public spending is the traditional public health measures of guaranteeing safe food, water, sanitation, drugs, and adequate regulation, as well as disseminating information to the public to encourage behavioral changes needed for long-term improvements in health outcomes. Such health promotion programs include the collection and dissemination of information on basic hygiene and the value of preventive care, such as anti-smoking, promotion of better nutrition, and appropriate measures to avoid contracting HIV-AIDS and other sexually transmitted diseases.

Third, the prevalence of infectious disease among the poor, the importance of the type of water source a family uses to child survival, and the high barriers between the poor and good sources of water and sanitation constitute additional empirical support that environmental/externality correcting interventions are of critical importance on both equity and efficiency

grounds. Figure 3.7 shows the effect that differential access to safe water and sanitation facilities has in explaining the difference in child (under two) mortality between the richest and poorest quintiles. The difference in mortality is 3.8 percentage points (3 percent versus 6.8 percent) in urban areas and 3.43 percent in rural areas. Of these, for the urban areas 1.3 percentage point are attributable to differential patterns of water sources, with another 0.4 percentage point attributable to different patterns of sanitation. For the rural areas the equivalent numbers are 0.73 percentage points of the 3.43-point difference attributable to water and 0.2 percentage point for sanitation. In other words, if poor people had the water and sanitation facilities of the rich, the gap between their mortality and that of the rich would be lower by 45 percent (1.3 + 0.4)/3.8 in urban areas and 26.5 percent (0.73 + 0.2)/3.4 in rural areas.

The jump from these results to policy implications is not straightforward. While it is very important to extend water and sanitation coverage, it is not necessarily important to do this by public expenditure. The pattern of access indicates that current subsidies for water and sanitation are highly regressive. This "average" incidence of expenditure would call for raising charges for these services and thereby reducing the amount of subsidy going to them. However, expansion of the use of better water and sanitation facilities would benefit the relatively poor and thus has a "marginal" incidence that is progressive. These seemingly opposing considerations can be reconciled by noting that research in India and many other places in the world has found a high enough willingness to pay for safe, reliable water and sanitation services and that services with appropriate

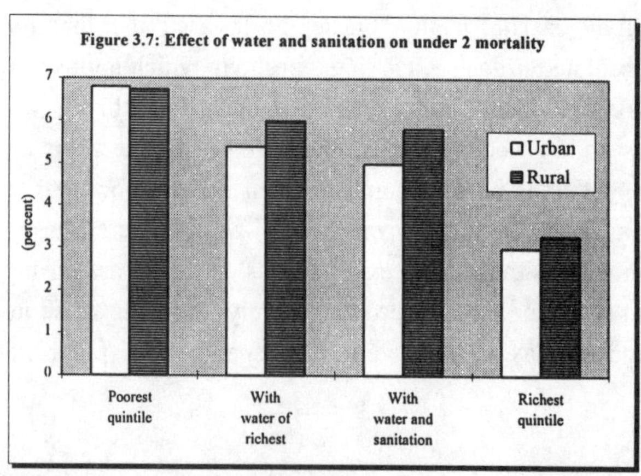

charges can be extended with small net public spending. However, basic health education concerning hygiene, washing of hands, and the value and appropriate use of water is a critical feature of public health services and should therefore be financed out of public funds.

Fourth, because public facilities are equitably distributed, they could be a powerful channel through which to offer the poor a form of insurance. The rural poor must often meet the financial burden of medical emergencies through debt, distress sale of real assets, or reductions in food or other important consumption items, sacrifices which are very real but may not show up in health status at all. In addition the poor tend to use both inpatient and outpatient services in public hospitals because they are free and because the quality of service offered at PHCs is poor. This is confirmed by earlier studies (World Bank 1995b) and Figure 3.8 showing that public provision for inpatient care at hospitals reflects a high degree of equity since people in the lowest expenditure quintiles are at least as likely to receive subsidized care as those in the higher-income expenditure brackets. In almost all states, for both rural and urban areas, hospitalized episodes reported by the lowest expenditure classes were more likely to be treated in government facilities. Against this background, subsidizing the provision of medical care may serve an important insurance function, with the benefits expected to be potentially higher for the poor than for the non-poor (see Annex 3.2 for the details of how the value of this insurance is estimated). This study estimates the welfare gain that would come from subsidized hospital care—on top of the value of the service itself in medical terms—to be in the range of 40 to 70 percent of the costs of providing the service to patients in the lowest 40

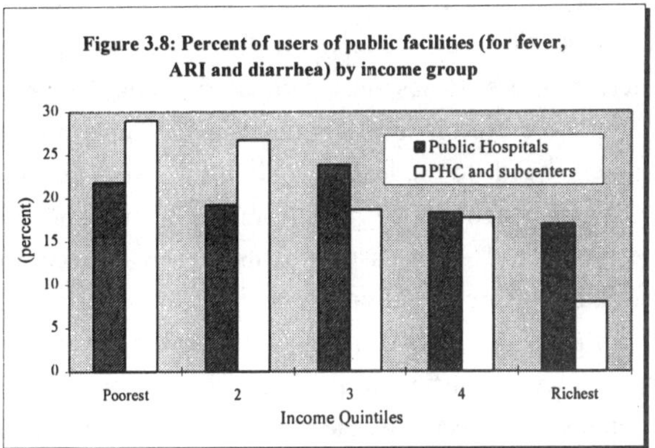

Figure 3.8: Percent of users of public facilities (for fever, ARI and diarrhea) by income group

percent of the population, people for whom insurance is not a realistic option. Figures 3.9 and 3.10 show this value increasing with the cost of the service—reflecting the need for insurance for relatively expensive treatment. They also show it decreasing with income, reflecting the greater capacity of richer people to absorb any given sudden expenditures. Finally, the value of the insurance relative to the cost of providing it goes down with the likelihood of the condition. That is, it is cheaper to insure rare events for the value of insurance offered.

However, whether public provision of such treatment is a progressive expenditure depends critically on the referral system. If the referral system is such that access to expensive hospital care is based on medical need, this is potentially a great boon to the poor. If the referral system cannot assure this and access to free care depends on income and social status rather than need, then expansion of hospital-based services will be regressive. India is fortunate to have a pattern of public hospital use that is relatively equitable, in contrast to many other developing countries. This serves as a strong base from which protection against the risk of financial loss can be successfully offered to the poor. The potential benefits

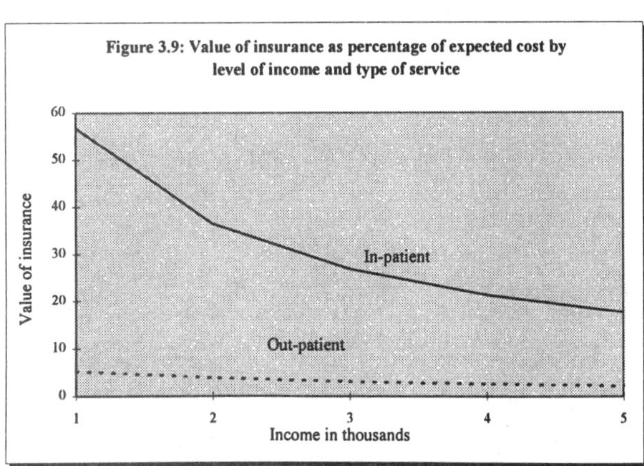

Figure 3.9: Value of insurance as percentage of expected cost by level of income and type of service

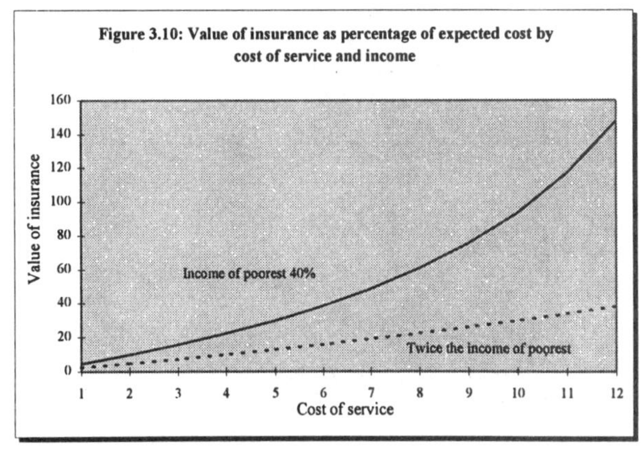

Figure 3.10: Value of insurance as percentage of expected cost by cost of service and income

can be enhanced further if the current problems of transportation and communication are solved to increase access to hospitals, particularly in rural areas.

These are obviously issues which India's policy makers need to address. This study showed the potential benefit to the poor from public subsidies to hospital care. India's policy makers will need to evaluate this option against other possible alternatives and choose what services they will be willing to ensure against and what type of provision they would like to promote. For example, the provision of medical care as an insurance mechanism does not have to be provided through publicly managed hospitals. The poor could be equally well served by public financing of private provision of services in rural areas, by a major effort to increase the quality of care through training, incentives, and regulation, or by community-based insurance schemes. Further research is urgently needed, however, to underpin the necessary reforms to both public and private health systems in India and further guide the determination of the major policy directions.

The discouraging results regarding the effectiveness of subcenters and PHCs, combined with the preceding analysis of the potential benefits of hospital care for the poor, raise some questions about conventional wisdom in health policy. In international health discussions the primary health care model of service delivery is a standard prescription. In the Indian context this should be assessed against the practical issues of implementation. Publicly provided, simple, and relatively inexpensive curative care could be a good policy only if the problems of managing such a vast, decentralized system of medical services can be solved. The perennial problems of posting doctors and other personnel in poor or remote areas, of maintaining an adequate supply of medicines and other materials, and providing sufficient supervision to ensure diligence on the part of health workers remain. Yet they need to be solved if public expenditures are to have their intended redistributive impact. Similarly, hospital care is a progressive use of public expenditures only if the referral system assures equitable access. Thus policy prescriptions need to be evaluated against a realistic assessment of the ability to manage and implement them.

Finally, policy should be pragmatic and driven by what really works. There is a need for serious evaluation of programs and investments to understand fully the factors that influence the performance of health systems. A basic requirement, for instance, for ensuring good allocation of public expenditures is to determine whether policies have their intended effect. Assessing the actual impact of public policy—how much of the subsidy reaches the poor and how valuable it is to them—is seriously hampered by lack of relevant evidence. The available data does not lend itself to such an evaluation. Since there is such a large private sector, the impact of any public action has to be assessed on the population as a whole. Wider coverage of public facilities may have a large effect on quality access to care by the poor or may simply replace private care. This can only be found out by assessments of health status before and after such expansion and not by inward-looking assessments of the care given in public clinics alone. Better regular studies of health status and services can help direct resources to where they are most useful. They can also help to keep policy makers focused on the real-life effects of their policies.

Introduction

India's anti-poverty programs, the 1997 Poverty Assessment found, have at best partial success in reaching their intended beneficiaries. In the Integrated Child Development Services (ICDS) many poor are not covered, while one in five of those helped are non-poor. In some others, such as the Public Distribution System (PDS), the proportion can reach three out of five. Additionally, better-performing programs are often under-funded; complex and costly administration results in many schemes carrying delivery costs higher than the value of the resulting benefits; ill-defined and multiple objectives reduce quality and accountability; and inadequate monitoring often uses indicators that distort programs' true objectives. Drawing on the 1993-94 NSS, this chapter provides new empirical evidence of the incidence of the PDS, Integrated Rural Development Program (IRDP), and public works programs on per capita consumption. Results of qualitative assessments from districts in UP and Bihar, two of India's poorest states, are also used to add to the ongoing efforts of evaluating the impacts of public spending on some of India's wide array of anti-poverty programs. The analysis suggests that the poor benefit more, on average, from public works programs than the non-poor, that the non-poor continue to benefit significantly from the other programs as well as from public works.

That evidence amounts to an urgent call to reexamine India's safety net strategy and—based on that scrutiny—to devise and fund a streamlined approach that makes the best use of scarce funds and delivers the most help to those most in need. This chapter proposes options to target more effectively the food subsidy as well as the public works programs. Options to redesign the IRDP are taken up in the forthcoming Rural Finance Report.

Background: Government anti-poverty programs

As a portion of the total central budget, estimated expenditures on the eight categories of officially classified anti-poverty programs detailed in Table 4.1 have increased from over 5 percent in 1990–91 to close to 7 percent in 1997-98. If spending on basic needs program is added, central government spending was close to 9 percent in 1997-98. Typically state-level spending adds an additional 25 to 50 percent. The initiatives range from food and kerosene subsidies to child health and nutrition efforts, as well as job-creating public works programs and small loans for rural households. Their variety is more impressive than their effectiveness in reducing poverty.

The PDS, to start with the oldest and costliest single program, distributes rice, wheat, edible oil, kerosene, and sugar at subsidized prices through a network of some 400,000 fair-price shops in urban and rural areas throughout India. Its total subsidies have

	Food subsidy[a]	Rural employment programs[b]	IRDP and related	Social welfare & nutrition	NRY	Welfare of SC/STs	Total center APP	Center APP and basic needs[c]
1990-91	2.3	1.9	0.4	0.3	0.1	0.3	5.3	6.4
1991-92	2.6	1.6	0.3	0.4	0.1	0.4	5.3	6.6
1992-93	2.3	2.1	0.3	0.4	0.1	0.4	5.6	6.7
1993-94	3.9	2.8	0.5	0.4	0.1	0.4	8.0	9.4
1994-95	3.2	2.9	0.4	0.9	0.0	0.5	7.9	9.3
1995-96	3.0	2.7	0.4	0.8	0.0	0.4	7.3	8.9
1996-97	3.0	2.5	0.3	0.7	0.0	0.4	7.0	8.9
1997-98	3.2	2.3	0.2	0.7	0.0	0.3	6.7	8.9

Table 4.1: Central plan budgetary expenditures on anti-poverty programs: 1990–91 to 1997–98 (percent of total expenditure)

a. Non-plan expenditure.

b. Includes JRY, EAS, Indira Awas Yojana, and Million Wells Schemes.

c. Basic needs programs include outlays for elementary education, adult education, accelerated rural water supply program, rural sanitation, urban water supply and sanitation, child welfare (include midday meals program), backward area development programs (drought prone, desert, wastelands).

Source: Based on Government data.

stabilized at around 0.5 percent of GDP in recent years. If the PDS functions as designed, consumers are protected against price fluctuations in the open market, farmers are shielded against excessive losses during periods of surplus, and in poor harvest years the public at large is cushioned against food shortages and famine.

Recognizing that the food subsidies often did not reach the poorest households, authorities introduced the targeted PDS (TPDS) in 1997 to link state-level allocations (and so the PDS subsidy) directly to each state's share of total population living below the official poverty line and to provide poor households with 10 kg of cereals each month at half the prevailing economic cost. Poor households are defined as those with income levels below the official poverty line (BPL) as distinct from APL (above poverty line) households. For the present APL households are permitted to purchase food grains and other goods at normal PDS prices, but these limited subsidies are to be gradually phased out. Early reports suggest that since the 1997 targeting, India's poorer states are receiving a substantially higher share of PDS subsidies. Wheat offtake in UP (one of the poorest and largest), for example, increased from 4.4 percent of the total (207.8 tons) in 1994-95 to an estimated 12.6 percent of the total (695.4 tons) in 1997-98. Bihar (another large, poor state) also increased its wheat offtake shares from 4.7 percent of the total (222.3 tons) to an estimated 7.5 percent (410.7 tons) over the same time period.

The ***Integrated Child Development Services*** (ICDS), a nutrition and child development scheme targeted at children up to the age of six, provides an integrated package of services including growth monitoring, health education for mothers, early childhood education, health checkups, immunization, and referral and supplemental feeding in a program aimed to attack the malnutrition-disease cycle by bringing nutritionally deprived children into the formal health system. Another important nutrition scheme is the midday meals program for school children. Significantly more extensive, it is also less well targeted than the ICDS. Other programs for tribal and scheduled castes provide a wide variety of services, ranging from cash and in-kind transfers to employment generation and investment projects. A *National Social Assistance Program (NSAP),* introduced in 1995, for the first time provides a mechanism for direct central government assistance to states in providing old-age pensions and survivor and maternity benefits.

Among the largest and best known of the numerous urban and rural employment programs are the *Jawahar Rojgar Yojana* (JRY) and the *Employment Assurance Scheme* (EAS), both designed primarily to help ensure gainful employment for poor households and contribute to the expansion of infrastructure and other social overhead capital in backward areas. In 1997-98, JRY and EAS received roughly equal levels of funding (0.14 percent of GDP) from the central budget, although the two are administratively very dissimilar. The JRY is administratively complex. Of its total funds, 75 percent are earmarked for various rural infrastructure schemes (i.e., the Million Wells Scheme (MWS), housing construction under the Indira Awas Yojana—both targeted to SC/ST households). The rest goes to social forestry projects. All, however, are allocated to the states according to a set formula based on the proportion of poor persons residing in each one. States in turn allocate JRY funds to districts based on population shares and an index of backwardness. From there JRY funds pass down to block and village level strictly according to population shares. Unique in its level of decentralization—work plans and contracts are administered by the village *panchayats*, subject to basic program guidelines and overall clearance of the work program by the District Rural Development Authority (DRDA)—the JRY generates an estimated one billion days of employment each year, an achievement which translates into the likely participation of some 30 to 40 percent of potential beneficiaries.

In contrast, EAS is demand driven. District authorities apply directly to its central administration for funding, and allocations are made based on the size and backwardness of blocks included in each district. Also, unlike the JRY, the District Collector/Deputy Commissioner (DC) has overall responsibility for coordinating work and allocating funds among blocks within the district.

Finally, India's IRDP is the country's most well-known credit-based anti-poverty scheme. To date the program has reached roughly 50 million families, annually providing between 2 and 2.5 million loans in recent years. The Development of Women and Children in Rural Areas (DWCRA), a subplan of the IRDP, specifically targets women (about 500,000 a year) in poor rural households. Another sub-plan of the IRDP—Training of Rural Youth for Self-Employment (TRYSE)—teaches technical and entrepreneurial skills to rural youth (300,000 annually). The credit portion of the IRDP, which is administered through the banking system, is purpose-specific, charges centrally fixed interest rates, and includes a subsidy on loan principal.

How much do the poor benefit from these poverty programs?

A wealth of governmental and other studies of India's wide array of anti-poverty programs provided the raw material for last year's poverty report. The data ranged from research that drew on very small samples and often used mainly beneficiary assessment techniques (focus groups, rapid appraisal) to a few larger-scale and more rigorous inquiries (e.g., National Council of Applied Economic Research [NCAER] and earlier work using the 1986-87 NSS—at least on PDS). Most of these studies found that the poor are not well served by existing anti-poverty programs. This chapter, while providing new empirical backing for those conclusions, goes a step further. It attempts to (i) measure more rigorously and with more recent information the success of three anti-poverty programs in reaching the poor, and (ii) better understand the processes and systemic factors operating at the local level which may hinder or improve the performance of anti-poverty programs in particular and public services more generally.

Boxes 4.1 and 4.2 discuss two of the main approaches usually used to measure the benefits from public spending: the *benefit incidence* approach and a non-quantitative variant of the *behavioral* approach—also referred to as village studies. Typically the latter provides information which cannot always be easily distilled from larger-scale household surveys: a rounded perspective on the life of rural household, relationships with surrounding communities, and the role of village institutions. (The 1997 India Poverty Assessment discussed the contribution of village studies to the understanding of poverty determinants in India). The two methods complement each other, producing data and analyses that can better inform the debate on the effectiveness of public policies in reducing poverty. By refining average benefit incidence analysis, the findings of this report could enable policy makers to assess better the distributional impact of expanding or contracting a given anti-poverty program using the marginal odds of participation (MOP) (see below and Annex 4.1). The latter is an advance in understanding the effectiveness of public spending in reducing poverty.

India's NSS for 1993-94 contains data about household participation in three key programs: public works schemes (identifying household members who worked on one for at least 60 of the previous 365 days), the IRDP (for households receiving assistance during the last 5 years), and the PDS (for households making subsidized commodity purchases within the last 30 days). Collating data on such participation (while recognizing that such data are not very refined) with data on total consumption expenditure per person at the household level makes it possible to determine the current distribution of benefits from public spending across income groups in India (Box 4.1).

Table 4.2: Average participation rates for India's main anti-poverty programs in rural areas

	Public works programs		IPDP		PDS	
Quintile of expenditure per capita	Participation rate (%)	Average odds of participation (mean=1.0)	Participation rate (%)	Average odds of participation (mean=1.0)	Participation rate (%)	Average odds of participation (mean=1.0)
Poorest	5.0	1.23	6.5	1.03	69.5	0.92
2nd	4.6	1.13	7.1	1.13	76.7	1.01
3rd	4.2	1.04	6.4	1.03	77.9	1.03
4th	3.5	0.86	6.0	0.96	78.1	1.00
5th	3.4	0.83	5.6	0.89	76.1	1.00

Note: The table gives the average odds of participation, defined as the ratio of the quintile-specific participation rate to the overall mean for each program. Calculations based on the 1993-94 NSS.

The sample size (rural areas only) of the 1993-94 NSS was 61,464 households. The analysis is done at the level of the 62 NSS regions in 19 states (see Haque, Lanjouw, and Ravallion 1998).

Of these three main anti-poverty programs operating in rural India in 1993-94, new World Bank research that uses benefit incidence methodology (Lanjouw and Ravallion 1998) shows that the poorest quintile is well served by public works programs, with the credit program (IRDP) in second place and the food program (PDS) doing least well in reaching the poor. Even more significant in its consequences for public policy is the finding that a non-negligible share of non-poor benefit from even the public works programs. There is a need to investigate further who these non-poor are.

For both the public works programs and the IRDP (Table 4.2) participation rates fall as expenditure per person increases (movement from poorest to richest quintile). However, the rate of decline is not large; in public works programs the odds of the poorest quintile participating are 1.23 versus 0.83 for the richest quintile, and participation rates among the richest 20 percent in terms of consumption per person are high. The rate of decline is even lower for the IRDP, and as expected, the PDS participation rate is actually lowest for the poorest quintile and highest in the middle-expenditure quintile.

How much would spending reform benefit the poor?

To see how (or if) extra or reallocated spending under any of these programs would increase their reach to the poorest income groups, it is necessary to go beyond the widely used and informative average participation rates to estimate the likelihood that participation by the poor in a given program would increase more than proportionally if spending on that program rose. Table 4.3 presents the results of this analysis in terms of the MOP—or gain in per capita subsidy incidence for each quintile—in public works, IRDP, and PDS programs assumed to follow from a one Rupee increase in aggregate spending on each (see Annex 4.1 for calculation of the MOP). For both the public works programs and the IRDP, it is notable that the MOP tend to fall more steeply (Table 4.3) from the poorest to the richest quintiles than do the average odds (Table 4.2). The shift is less striking within the PDS.

This deeper look at the distribution of the benefits of these three anti-poverty programs reveals that by itself, a measurement of the *average* odds of participation underestimates how "pro-poor" a spending increase on one or another program would be (see van de Walle, 1998, Annex 4.1). The contrast is particularly dramatic for the IRDP, where the average odds of participation are marginally higher for the

---

Box 4.1: What is 'benefit incidence' analysis?

Benefit incidence analysis has become popular since the path-breaking work on Malaysia by Meerman (1979) and on Colombia by Selowsky (1979). A recent resurgence of interest in the approach has been reviewed in van de Walle and Nead (1995).

Benefit incidence analysis seeks to measure how government subsidies on anti-poverty programs and services such as health and education are distributed across groups in society. Two broad factors determine the distribution: the size and allocation of government spending and the behavior of beneficiary households. In the first category, the lower the spending and the greater the effective cost recovery, the lower will be the subsidy embodied in the service provided. For the second factor, distribution will depend on who uses the service that the government provides. It is only by using the service (for instance, participating in an anti-poverty program, sending a child to school, or using health facilities) that individuals and households can lay a claim to the in-kind transfer implicit in the subsidy. Benefit incidence analysis therefore brings together two sources of information: data on the government subsidy (estimated as the unit cost of providing the service less any cost recovery) allocated to the different categories of service (public works, schooling, inpatient hospital care, etc.); and information usually obtained from household surveys on the use of these services by individuals and households.

In general, government expenditures will be more equally distributed when the spending is concentrated on services used widely by the population, and especially by poorer groups. Thus outlays concentrated on primary education or on health care widely used by the poor tend to be more equally distributed than funds that go for services found not to be generally used by poorer groups.

Source: Demery 1997, van de Walle 1995.

poorest quintile than the richest (1.03 versus 0.89) but widely different (1.11 versus 0.39) in the MOP. When compared with the average odds of participation (as traditionally done in benefit incidence studies), the share of total IRDP spending imputed to the poorest 40 percent of the population is over 11 percent higher, while that imputed to the richest 20 percent is 56 percent lower. Similarly, while the average odds of participation in public works are higher for the poorest quintile than the richest (1.23 versus 0.83), the spread in the MOP (1.16 versus 0.55) is even wider. When compared to the average odds of participation, while the share of total spending on public works imputed to the poorest 40 percent of the population increases by over 4 percent, that imputed to the richest 20 percent falls by 28 percent. The poor would benefit more than what the average incidence would suggest from subsidies under either the IRDP or public works, while the non-poor would capture less. The conclusions from this analysis are that the marginal incidence of public works programs and the IRDP appears to be more progressive than the average incidence would suggest. The poor would benefit more than average and the non-poor even less.

Benefit incidence analysis provides a useful tool for assessing the quantitative distribution of benefits from public spending. The data broadly confirm the conclusion that public works programs perform best at reaching India's poorest, that the IRDP is more effective within the three middle quintiles (including those living at the poverty line—roughly the 40th percentile), and that food subsidies flow disproportionately to those least in need. The analysis therefore suggests that switching a significant share of

PDS funds to public works programs would benefit the poorest most. To refine these observations further, it is necessary to see how valid they are across India's diverse regions.

Regional distribution of benefits

Although some states have done far better than others at reaching the poor, the same states do not always perform well in all three programs and poor states do not necessarily achieve better results than wealthier ones. The wide variation in performance—as true of anti-poverty program as of investments in health and education—between states and across regions of India is typified by participation rates of the poorest 20 percent of rural households in public works programs in Orissa and Himachal Pradesh that are, respectively, almost three and well over four times higher than those of the richest 20 percent. For Maharashtra, the participation rates of the poorest 20 percent of households in both public works and the IRDP are higher than those of the richest 20 percent. At the other extreme, states such as AP, Gujarat, Kerala, and Tamil Nadu show the poorest quintile, with a below-average participation rate. Annex 4.2 gives a state-by-state breakdown of participation rates.

Since UP and Bihar are among the poorest and most populous states, India's anti-poverty programs should, if they were well targeted, achieve broad coverage and function effectively in both of them. That is not the case. Incidence analysis (Annex 4.2) shows, on the contrary, that public works programs and the IRDP are only marginally targeted toward the poor in Bihar, and that PDS is used by households across the

Table 4.3: Marginal odds of participation for India's anti-poverty programs			
Quintile	Public works programs	IRDP	PDS
Poorest	1.16	1.11	1.06
	(3.27)	(15.49)	(8.14)
2nd	0.93	1.28	0.99
	(3.64)	(17.73)	(7.26)
3rd	0.80	1.21	0.91
	(2.98)	(23.52)	(6.88)
4th	0.92	0.96	0.86
	(4.32)	(19.09)	(7.16)
5th	0.55	0.39	0.81
	(3.29)	(8.06)	(6.27)

Notes: The table gives the instrumental variables estimate of the regression coefficient of the quintile-specific program participation rates across regions on the average participation rate by state for that program, based on the 1993-94 NSS. The leave-out mean state participation rate is the instrument for the actual mean (see Annex 4.1 for details). The numbers in parentheses are t-ratios.

income distribution. In UP, only public works programs serve the poor more than the middle and upper classes; the IRDP is used more by the middle quintiles.

Village studies of poverty and the use of public programs recently undertaken in 30 villages located in southeastern UP and north and central Bihar (Box 4.2) complement quantitative incidence analysis with a rich and varied picture of poverty and the effectiveness of anti-poverty programs in some of India's poorest areas. Government programs that were cited as most visible and most beneficial to villagers in the sample communities included (i) schools, (ii) the PDS, (iii) drinking water schemes, and (iv) irrigation investments. In contrast, researchers found Anganwadi centers (ICDS) functioning in only a few of the study villages. In most, the aims of the ICDS were poorly understood, and in none did informants say that they had received any significant benefit from an

Anganwadi center. Supply of clean drinking water is seen as a major success of government action (primarily through the Minimum Needs Scheme). However, poor women are often still required to walk long distances to handpumps, and low-caste individuals must sometimes suffer humiliation when wells are located only in high-caste tolas.

The most extensively used of the anti-poverty programs, the PDS is nevertheless not well targeted toward the poor, a weakness that the advent of the TPDS in 1997 may be remedying. PDS fair-price stores existed in every village the study covered, but were nearly always to be found in the wealthier communities within the village, which may contribute to the diversion of the food subsidy to the non-poor.

Early evidence from the village studies suggests that targeting measures taken under the TPDS may have at least significantly increased the amount of PDS foodgrains reaching the poor. BPL lists had been developed in the majority of study villages and new ration cards (so-called red cards) actually distributed in over half of them. Many of the study respondents felt that most of the poor—particularly the very poor—were included on the lists, although researchers also heard numerous reports of inappropriate inclusion and exclusion. Nevertheless, the TPDS suffers from many of the same implementation problems as its predecessor, the PDS. For example, the poor said they were discouraged from using the PDS by irregular hours of store operation, lack of information about when rations would be available, insults from shopkeepers, and high transport costs relative to expected savings. Poor informants in UP complained that by the time they learn of a delivery, most of the grain has already been distributed to the (wealthier) households living near the shop. Sugar rations were rarely available, and many informants claimed to receive less than their full 10 kg allocation.

In contrast to the familiarity and near-universal dissatisfaction with the PDS, public awareness of the JRY and EAS programs as sources of employment opportunities for poor villagers varied according to location. In most of the study areas, informants did not know that the basic objective of these programs was to provide employment security for them. Instead villagers perceive the JRY and EAS as infrastructure

---

Box 4.2: PRA participants' perceptions of central government poverty-alleviation programs

A study of poverty in backward areas of UP and Bihar, initiated in early 1997, addressed a number of questions related to the key characteristics of poverty, its persistence, and the possible avenues of escape. In the qualitative phase of the study, PRA methods and semi-structured interviews were used in a sample of 30 villages located in three districts in south eastern UP (Allahabad, Gorakhpur, and Chatrapati Sahmuji Maharaj Nagar [CSMN]) and four districts in north central Bihar (Jehanabad, Vaishali, Munger, and Saharasa).

Included in the PRA instruments was a module on the *Use and Perceptions of Government Programs*, designed to elicit information on (i) respondents' awareness of their entitlements to anti-poverty programs and services, (ii) availability and functioning of various programs, and (iii) users' perceptions of benefits and perceived importance of these benefits to improve their welfare levels. The module was administered to focus groups within each village (consisting of individuals from very poor/lower caste households, individuals from better-off/upper caste households, and groups of poor women). Semistructured interviews were also carried out with lower income individuals to better understand their felt needs for education, health services, credit, employment, and food security and to better understand the barriers that prevent households from utilizing existing services.

projects to build roads, bridges, install hand pumps, and irrigate previously unproductive lands (through the Million Wells Scheme (MWS), previously part of the JRY). In several cases, housing for SC/STs had been built under the aegis of the JRY. As such, the programs were valued by the poor for improving village living conditions and access to outside employment. In Gorakhpur, where the JRY was seen as a program that had opened chances for new jobs for the rural poor—although women were generally excluded—interviewers heard reports of misuse of JRY funds by officials in some areas and in the EAS. Work on various projects was carried out by contractors using trucks and tractors instead of more labor-intensive approaches (Box 4.3).

Opinions on the IRDP are also mixed. The village studies in UP and Bihar—like the incidence analysis above—suggest that the IRDP does benefit poor households, but not those at the very bottom of the income distribution (i.e., the lowest quintile). The credit-based and income means-tested IRDP studied in Maharashtra, for instance, was found to be far less well targeted than the state's Employment Guarantee Scheme (Rural Finance Report). Given the general consensus that most but not all poor households were on the IRDP list, as were some of the non-poor, the benefit incidence analysis finding that IRDP funds went mostly to rural middle-income groups appears confirmed.

The village studies found that IRDP loans were virtually the only form of formal credit locally available to the poor. Village money lenders, an alternative source of credit but at premium interest rates (50 to 100 percent a year), tend to increase interest rates according to the borrower's urgency and desperation. Although few IRDP loans were reported in recent years, many people (poor and less poor alike) in the study areas had taken them at some point over the past 10 years. Few loan recipients, however, had acquired (and retained) productive assets. A high percentage of the loans underwrote consumption in the case of marriages, sickness, and other surplus expenditure. Numerous examples were cited of people imprisoned for defaulting on IRDP loans, and few respondents expressed interest in obtaining new ones. Overall, access to IRDP loans has generally led to

> **Box 4.3: Leakages to the non-poor under the public works programs**
>
> The instances of misuse of public works objectives also confirm the findings of the benefit incidence analysis. Since public works are meant to be self-targeting, its benefits to the poor should have been higher than those indicated in table 4.2. The low employment impact of the employment generation programs was pervasive across districts covered under the study. In Allahabad District, for example, the EAS was carrying out construction in only one village, designated an Ambedkar village. However, there was more activity reported under the JRY. Handpumps had been installed and village roads were being constructed or repaired in all the villages under the JRY, but little work had taken place during the past two years. In Bihar, village pathways and roads had been constructed, but rarely by laborers from the village itself. In CSMN (previously Banda) District, wells had been repaired and bridges built, but again among those interviewed, none said they had received employment under these schemes. In CSMN District, the researchers were told that one Pradhan had recorded that a project had been executed in a scheduled tribe *basti* (locality) when in fact it had been carried out in his own upper-caste *basti*. In another reported instance, villagers who had performed some work under these programs had not been paid for it. In the Allahabad villages, women opined that employment under these schemes is provided only for the Pradhan's personal supporters or workers willing to sign for higher wages than those they actually received.

more indebtedness rather than sustained income generation, and as with public works programs, the IRDP has experienced significant leakages to the non-poor, particularly officials (Box 4.4).

Because the 1993-94 NSS did not include questions on participation in such anti-poverty programs as the *ICDS* and other rural infrastructure programs, it has not been possible to extend the benefit incidence analysis of the previous section to these programs. Most evaluations concluded that the performance of the program has been mixed. Program objectives are ambitious, resources are limited, and services are often stretched thin. Evidence from UP and Bihar indicates that public awareness of the ICDS is low. The reasons cited for the failure of the ICDS to operate were strikingly similar across regions—lack of training of Anganwadi workers and inadequate

Box 4.4: Diverting IRDP funds to the non-poor

Reports of corruption and payoffs to middlemen were pervasive, and few households claimed to have utilized loans for productive purposes. For instance, a review of the experience of 394 poor households in Bankura District in West Bengal found various kinds of misconduct under the IRDP that penalized the target group.   Banks in the sample improperly deducted 10 percent of the loan as charges, and most beneficiaries were told or perceived that they did not have to repay the loan portion.

Additionally, middlemen "captured" subsidies of credit-based anti-poverty programs, effectively increasing the cost of such transactions. A sampling of 312 "weak" borrowers in Tamil Nadu, turned up "incidental expenses" and "speed/quick or push money" amounting to Rs. 21 for every Rs. 100 of subsidy.   About two-thirds of this sample also reported "working" for the subsidy and producing "quick money" in addition to covering normal expenses.   Such "fixed" transaction costs, even if legitimate, were not only high but inherently regressive as well.

In another case study (Gangajalghati and Ranibandh), almost no IRDP beneficiary satisfied the eligibility criteria.   Their participation in the program came about through political interference; lack of proper information systems, and decisions by some bank officials to ignore poor repayment records, among other reasons.   Once the program participants obtained the loan in the form of goats, the animals were sold and the proceeds used for other purposes. Further, the shortage of goats in the area was such that the planned number of goat loans could not be met. Other schemes like blacksmithing and carpentry faced such difficulties as scant supplies of raw materials and the absence of proper marketing facilities.

Source: Rural Finance Report, World Bank, 1998.

financing and supervision, as well as misuse, of state-allocated funds and food supplies.   Recruitment practices were also criticized. For example, in some cases the daughters-in-law of rich families were recruited for a task they could not perform because they remain veiled whenever they are outside their homes.   Despite extensive spending on them, Anganwadi centers almost everywhere were found to be falling short as providers of early childhood education.

Weaknesses were identified in the implementation of the program in many locations. Over one-third of Anganwadi Women Worker (AWW), for example, were found to be unable to perform the growth monitoring function that is critical to identifying children in need of supplemental nutrition. Although Auxiliary Nurse Midwife (ANM) provided immunization support to 80 percent of Anganwadis, few received support in identifying children at risk or health education. In some cases an overburdened and undertrained AWW has had to neglect such key services as outreach or health education to fulfill the basic feeding, weighing, and childhood education requirements of her position. The synergistic character of the ICDS program suffers when any of its components is short-changed or abandoned. Other studies have concluded that children spend most of their time sitting or sleeping, crowded into a dark room with little preschool education provided (Martorell 1997). And the program as a whole is bypassing those most vulnerable: children under the age of two and pregnant women.

While not functioning as a part of India's food security system because grain rations of 3 kilos each month are too low and supplies are not linked to needs or shortages, the ***midday meals program*** does appear to be providing an incentive for poor households to send their children to school.

What reforms can best reduce non-poor capture of program benefits?

Reforming anti-poverty programs. The twin pillars of India's strategy for reducing poverty are accelerated and sustained labor-intensive growth and investment in developing human capital.   Designed to provide supplementary but important support to that central effort, the various anti-poverty programs consume significant resources but yield little gain in raising the living standards of the poor.   Because of the unsustainable fiscal cost and the disappointing performance in reaching the poor, the government already has started to look at options for streamlining functioning and targeting. Such is the intent of the TPDS and the recommendations for reforms contained in the approach paper to the Ninth five-year Plan.

The reform options suggested in the approach paper, however, are too modest. They envision only marginal improvements in the cost-effectiveness of anti-poverty programs that beg for a thorough going overhaul. Three kinds of flaws, in particular, need to be remedied. *First*, the programs are still burdened by multiple and sometimes conflicting objectives between serving the poor, stabilizing commodity prices, or building rural roads. *Second,* the problems that the programs are designed to address (i.e., widespread poverty, malnutrition, mass illiteracy) are too massive to be resolved through public resources allocated to these programs, however efficient resource use is. *Third,* many anti-poverty programs have become highly politicized. India's complex socio-political environment makes it very difficult to change existing programs, as shown during the effort to reform the PDS.

Anti-poverty program failures: the non-poor go to the head of the line, the poor to the back. Describing what has gone wrong makes it easier to suggest directions for reform. The benefit incidence analysis set out in this chapter, for instance, suggests that the non-poor have been able to capture significant shares of the resources flowing through these programs while the poor, the intended beneficiaries, only begin to participate as spending rises. The geographic pattern of participation by quintile suggests that although high marginal gains to the poor emerge later, the non-poor tend to be the first to benefit when a program is introduced. This skewed result is due either to imperfect targeting or to varying costs. In the first case, the government either lacks the information and incentive structure to target perfectly or finds it politically not feasible to risk eroding the crucial support of the non-poor through perfect targeting of the poor. The second factor applies when costs and benefits of program participation vary with the scale of the program and its location. Social programs invariably impose various costs on participants, such as cofinancing through fees, transport costs, or opportunity cost of participating in public programs by attending a nutrition center or sending a child to school, or hidden costs such as bribes paid to secure access to programs. Since poor areas are often more remote, initial placement there will tend to be lower.

The results from the surveys on the social and economic determinants of poverty in India's most backward rural areas—southern and eastern UP and north and central Bihar—confirm the conclusions above in three broad findings. *First*, overwhelming evidence shows that many of the resources intended to be spent on anti-poverty programs have been diverted to serve the needs of the rural elites (Boxes 4.3 and 4.4). *Second*, the expected positive impacts of decentralization on targeting and effectiveness of anti-poverty programs have yet to be fully realized in the study areas. Poorer/lower-caste members of the community, who felt they had far more knowledge in the choice of what would benefit them most, still lacked the political power to shift spending patterns to their benefit. *Third*, an ongoing economic—and to some extent, social—transformation in the study regions has caused the poor to depend more rather than less on government-financed safety nets and welfare schemes. The absolute ascendancy of the upper castes is slowly being eroded; the traditional or *jajmani* system is on the wane; attached labor is now less common than free (casual) labor in many of the areas studied. Many of the poor now aspire to jobs outside the village and outside the land-based agriculture sector. While this freedom allows casual laborers to negotiate with various employees and to seek higher wages, it has also shrunk credit opportunities (e.g., from landlords) and other traditional safety nets within the village. Not only do the poor look more to government for social protection, but government's ability to respond to these needs may have an important role in facilitating this economic transition.

Options for reform

Safety nets have a key role in achieving poverty reduction, but India urgently needs to formulate an anti-poverty strategy that is fiscally sustainable. To increase their cost-effectiveness and extend their outreach to the really poor, safety nets need to be targeted to those who cannot participate in the growth process because of physical handicaps combined with poverty or continuing exposure to uninsured risk. Further research in this area is crucially needed to design such a strategy. The findings of the average benefit incidence analysis suggest that the poor are highly represented among the beneficiaries of public works programs. Expanding such programs further (preferably through a reallocation of spending away from the less effective poverty programs) would increase the benefits to the poor more than the average incidence suggests. The marginal incidence analysis, by making it possible to assess the distributional impacts of changes in the levels and allocations of spending on the three anti-poverty programs, provides the beginning for a firm foundation for building safety net programs that can, through effective targeting to the genuinely needy, make them fiscally sustainable. Effective targeting need not be exclusive. Some level of slip-over to the non-poor is unavoidable if political support for such programs is to be maintained.

To be effective, safety nets need to be part of policies for human capital development. The effectiveness of public policies in reducing poverty and household exposure to risk depends to a large extent on policy actions in other areas. The evidence in this report shows that poor households lack access to basic social services crucial to their capacity to contribute and benefit from growth through higher productivity and earnings. Their children are less likely to be in school (Chapter 2), more likely to be malnourished, and more prone to life-threatening diseases (Chapter 3). Yet as this report shows, spending on primary education could be more effective in reducing poverty than any of the anti-poverty programs. Giving a mother primary education may do more, studies show, to raise her child's nutritional status than providing food subsidies to raise household food intake. All these findings bring into sharp focus the fact that the effectiveness of safety nets in protecting the poor depends heavily on that of the delivery of such crucial services as education, water and sanitation, and public health, which are not strictly part of the safety nets. In addition, even actions such as improving the cost-effectiveness of food-based transfers that are part of the safety net systems are also dependent on improving the functioning of food markets to increase supply and lower prices so that poor households, among others, gain greater food security.

Sustained, labor-intensive economic growth and accessible, good-quality health care and education are,

as previous chapters of this report argued, key policy ingredients of any effective, long-term anti-poverty strategy. As to short-run actions to reduce the insecurity of poor households, it is urgent to consolidate all existing central- and state-sponsored schemes into a single, two-faceted approach (i) one public works program à la the JRY or EAS and (ii) food-linked transfers (experimenting with alternative transfer channels such as the TPDS, possibly the ICDS, or the public works and social security programs). For the rest, some of the costliest and less effective anti-poverty programs need to be eliminated; others could be merged into these two subcomponents.

Since unemployment insurance was not a feasible way of dealing with rural unemployment, India used labor-intensive public works programs to steer income to households at risk. These programs have less exacting financial requirements than unemployment insurance schemes and limited disincentive effects, and they are comparatively easy to administer (partly because they are based on a simple "self-selection" mechanism). India would therefore gain by keeping such programs but consolidating them into a single public works venture along the lines of the JRY or EAS (Box 4.5), whether its aim is to reach the poor in rural or in urban areas.

The usefulness of keeping the DWCRA as a credit-based anti-poverty program should be re-examined in light of the proposal to reform the IRDP and rural credit markets (Rural Finance Report 1998), Training of Rural Youth for Self-Employment (TRYSEM) and Scheme of Urban Wage Employment (SUWE) should be integrated with education and vocational training and no longer managed as safety net programs. All other "public works" type programs such as schemes for urban wage employment, Nehru Rozgar Yojana (NRY), Indira Awas Yojana (IAY), SHASU, and MWS, should be consolidated into either a JRY- or EAS-type workfare scheme (Table 4.4). Political considerations excepted, this cost-effective consolidation—if PRIs manage the programs at the local level—should in fact simplify their implementation and monitoring by a single agency. It should help to reduce red tape, administrative and monitoring overhead, and the costs of targeting, since the task of monitoring eligibility is likely to be more feasible and less costly at the local level with community participation.

Food-linked transfer programs

Retargeted PDS. Recent government efforts to retarget the previously universally provided food subsidy (on rice and wheat) to those below the poverty line is a step in the right direction as far as targeting is concerned. While there is some evidence that the poor are gaining, TPDS will probably continue to subsidize the non-poor as well. One drawback that invites abuse and diversion of grains from the poor to the non-poor under the current TPDS is the expectation that the retail dealer will supply the same variety of grain at half price to the poor (theoretically those with ration cards) and at the regular price to the non-poor. Given past experience with similar arrangements for kerosene and cooking oil (Radhakrishna and Subbarao 1997), it is unrealistic to expect anything but high levels of fraud. Although the central government plans to enforce strict monitoring, such control is likely to be difficult and administratively costly.

There are increasing calls within India to choose only those foods most consumed by the poor (such as coarse grains and unrefined sugar) as transfer instruments for the poor. The evidence is, however, mixed. Results from the qualitative surveys carried out in four states in India in 1996 and more recently in Bihar and UP show that the poor produce rather than actually buy these commodities, which are not widely marketed. In addition, the short shelf life of coarse cereals makes storage problematical, and government intervention in the unregulated coarse-grain market would not be desirable. When all these considerations are combined with the evidence from the benefit incidence analysis, the highest gains to the poor would seem to come from (i) subsidizing only rice, wheat, and kerosene (for environmental considerations) under the TPDS; (ii) phasing out completely the second and untargeted channel of the PDS; and (iii) shifting progressively more public spending from food subsidies to public works programs.

While better targeting will help improve cost-effectiveness of food subsidy programs, it will not be sufficient by itself. The transfer mechanisms under

---

Box 4.5: What makes a good workfare scheme?

Experience with workfare schemes for poverty reduction in India has been diverse: some have proved effective in raising incomes of the poorest and at times of need, others have been far less effective. To achieve the potential for this class of anti-poverty interventions it is recommended that:

- The wage rate should be set at a level which is no higher than the prevailing market wage for unskilled manual labor in the setting in which the scheme is introduced.
- Restrictions on eligibility should be avoided; willingness to work at this wage rate should ideally be the only requirement for eligibility.
- If rationing is required (because demand for work exceeds the budget available at the wage set), then the program should be targeted to poor areas, as indicated by a credible "poverty map." However, flexibility should be allowed in future budget allocations across areas, to reflect differences in demand for the scheme.
- The labor intensity (share of wage bill in total cost) should be higher than normal for similar projects in the same setting. How much higher will depend on the relative importance attached to immediate income gains versus (income and other) gains to the poor from the assets created.
- The projects should be targeted to poor areas and should try to assure that the assets created are of value to poor people in those areas. Any exceptions—in which the assets largely benefit the non-poor—should require cofinancing from the beneficiaries, with such funds going back into the budget of the scheme.
- Performance should be monitored by use of careful independent evaluations.

Source: Ravallion 1998.

---

which such subsidies are delivered to the target group matter as well. The study by Radhakrishna and Subbarao (1997) identifies a number of transfer channels under which the food subsidy program could be made more cost-effective. The study recommends *first* a reduced role for the Food Corporation of India (FCI), with government controls over grain markets as well as procurement operations being phased out. The FCI could be allowed to compete in the market and could (because of its scale), over time, become an effective player in the market. Its new role could be to stabilize the price of foodgrains within a band and to maintain strategic buffer stocks or equivalent foreign exchange. *Second*, the subsidy cost saving (as the FCI goes out of procurement operations) could be distributed to PRIs in the form of food stamps or vouchers or as a conditional cash grant. The poor—identified by the PRIs—could be given these vouchers to be exchanged for food or, if resold, to make an equally worthwhile cash transfer. Another easy-to-implement option would be to link the food voucher program with other programs such as the JRY/EAS or a nutrition program such as the ICDS in regions where it is working. These measures are most likely to ensure targeting without incurring additional costs. At the same time, the poor may be given some choice in the type of grains they want to purchase as well as the retail outlets they patronize so as to preclude shop keepers' discriminating against lower castes—a practice identified in qualitative surveys as an obstacle between the poor and their share of subsidized food.

While the poor would benefit from better targeting of subsidies, they and India would benefit even more from a comprehensive **reform of agricultural policies** as discussed in Chapter 1. Such change is essential to broaden the base of growth, increase agricultural productivity, and improve the living standards of India's poor, of whom the vast majority live and work in rural areas.

As discussed earlier in this chapter, the ICDS should be strengthened to become a truly effective ECD program. For years the ICDS has focused on promoting cognitive development in children three to five years of age. As with Head Start in the United States, judging its success based on existing evaluations studies is difficult (Martorell 1997). Efforts are currently underway both to increase the program's cost-effectiveness and to widen coverage. However, widening coverage should not be identified with universalization of the program, as currently proposed by the authorities. Considerable scope still exists for expanding community participation in the management of the program and monitoring its impact and benefits. There is also a need to reexamine the usefulness of having both the AWW and subcenter health worker carrying out the same functions of health education and nutrition.

A forthcoming World Bank review of India's nutrition programs will suggest specific reforms to consolidate the many nutrition programs (including the PDS and midday meals program) and align them to advance a more coherent nutrition strategy along the malnutrition causality model disseminated by UNICEF. The study proposes a *radical* restructuring of the ICDS on the grounds that incremental changes in the areas of training, supervision, monitoring, and

Table 4.4: Centrally sponsored social security schemes * (Rs. billion at current prices)						
	1992-93	1993-94	1994-95	1995-96	1996-97	1997-98
Jawahar Rozgar Yojana (JRY)	25.46	33.06	35.35	29.55	16.55	19.53
Indira Awas Yojana (IAY)	..	..	..	4.92	11.94	11.44
Million Wells Scheme (MWS)	..	..	..	2.11	3.88	3.73
Employment Assurance Scheme (EAS)	..	6.00	11.40	18.16	18.40	19.05
Integrated Rural Development Programme (IRDP)	3.76	6.17	6.25	6.40	5.90	5.16
Training of Rural Youth for Self-Employment (TRYSEM)	0.08	0.08	0.09	0.14	0.14	0.46
Development of Women and Children in Rural Areas (DWCRA)	0.13	0.21	0.31	0.65	0.65	0.62
Nehru Rozgar Yojana [a] (NRY)	0.71	0.75	0.70	0.68	0.50	0.31
PM's Integrated Urban Poverty Eradication Program	..	..	..	1.00	0.71	0.32
Swarna Jayanti Shahari Rojgar Yojana (SJSRY)	..	..	..	..	..	1.03
Scheme of Urban Wage Employment	0.01	..	..	..	..	..
Public Distribution System (Total Civil Supplies)	0.18	0.18	0.41	1.49	0.99	0.42
Food Subsidy (PDS)	28.00	55.37	51.00	53.77	60.66	75.00
Supplementary Nutrition Program	0.25	..	..	..	..	..
Midday Meal Scheme	..	..	..	6.12	8.00	10.70
Integrated Child Development Services (ICDS)	4.01	4.73	5.37	6.69	6.82	8.35
Total	62.57	106.55	110.88	131.68	135.14	156.12

* All numbers are revised estimates.

Source: Union Budget, Expenditure Budget volume II, various years.

evaluation, vital as they are, will not be sufficient to overcome the basic structural inconsistency of the ICDS. The scheme seeks to carry out two quite distinct sets of tasks in one program with one worker—too many objectives and too few instruments. Given the choices available to address this problem, provision of a second worker, the study concludes, appears to be the most cost-effective option. Savings gained from shifting resources, for example, from the PDS to the ICDS (Levinson 1998) can finance this additional worker, the study argues. Other alternatives under consideration include community financing of part of the ICDS cost and reducing the food costs, which represent around 70 percent of ICDS unit cost, as the Tamil Nadu nutrition program has successfully done. The forthcoming study also suggests supplementing ICDS formal, center-based activities with home visits. A cadre of workers—well trained and linked to women's groups and schools—could assist nutrition and health personnel in promoting effective solutions to nutritional and health needs while fostering psychosocial development (Martorell 1997).

All suggestions for reform need to be grounded in solid cost-benefit analysis for each option before specific recommendations for change can be fully endorsed. It is important to avoid adding new programs to correct the inefficiencies of existing ones which, in India as elsewhere, are notoriously difficult to abolish or change. Before deciding on any alternative, the following questions need to be answered: Can home visits be more effective than center-based ones? Can good nutrition be best provided by ensuring adequate food distribution, providing food stamps, making food-for-work programs available, or improving general adult literacy programs, particularly for women? Are school feeding programs preferable to mothers' education programs as more effective means of promoting nutrition?

Conclusion. Anti-poverty programs that either do not reach the poor or that bestow a disproportionate share of their benefits on the non-poor are programs in urgent need of reform. The majority of India's safety net initiatives are misusing scarce financial resources that could be best invested to increase the poor's access to health and education services that have been shown to equip them to help themselves. Reform is not needed for its own sake but for the sake of India's poor and in the interests of having them both contribute to the growth process and benefit from it.

ANNEXES

Table 1: State poverty rates									
	Total			Rural			Urban		
State	HCI	PGI	SPGI	HCI	PGI	SPGI	HCI	PGI	SPGI
Punjab	11.46	1.84	0.46	11.69	1.90	0.48	10.90	1.69	0.40
Andhra Pradesh	21.87	4.54	1.48	15.89	2.88	0.86	38.82	9.27	3.20
Gujarat	24.15	4.77	1.42	22.16	4.07	1.16	28.28	6.22	1.96
Kerala	25.12	5.59	1.86	25.38	5.61	1.84	24.31	5.53	1.88
Haryana	25.22	4.94	1.51	28.26	5.60	1.74	16.47	3.05	0.85
Rajasthan	27.46	5.62	1.72	26.40	5.21	1.55	31.02	7.00	2.24
Himachal Pradesh	28.58	5.19	1.50	30.36	5.55	1.61	9.26	1.25	0.26
Karnataka	32.91	7.73	2.69	30.11	6.27	2.01	39.90	11.36	4.36
Tamil Nadu	35.40	8.33	3.00	32.95	7.30	2.49	39.92	10.23	3.92
Maharashtra	36.82	9.61	3.65	37.91	9.28	3.34	34.99	10.15	4.15
West Bengal	36.94	7.42	2.21	41.18	8.29	2.45	22.95	4.55	1.41
Assam	41.09	7.46	2.00	44.91	8.21	2.20	7.93	0.92	0.22
Uttar Pradesh	41.55	10.23	3.50	42.32	10.37	3.53	35.10	9.03	3.26
Madhya Pradesh	42.46	10.40	3.68	40.75	9.48	3.26	48.08	13.43	5.05
Orissa	48.64	11.89	4.10	49.81	11.96	4.07	40.64	11.41	4.29
Bihar	55.15	13.83	4.77	57.95	14.66	5.06	34.84	7.86	2.63
All India	36.13	8.42	2.86	37.07	8.43	2.80	33.06	8.38	3.07

Note: HCI: Head count index; PGI: Poverty Gap Index; SPGI: Squared Poverty Gap Index.
Source: Tabulations from Haque, Lanjouw, and Ravallion 1998.

Table 2: Proportion literate aged 7+, 1993-94									
	Total			Male			Female		
State	Urban	Rural	Total	Urban	Rural	Total	Urban	Rural	Total
Kerala	93.4	91.0	91.6	96.8	94.4	95.0	90.2	89.8	88.5
Asssam	87.6	68.3	70.4	92.0	76.4	78.1	82.6	58.5	61.2
Maharashtra	82.9	58.9	68.1	90.0	72.7	79.5	75.0	44.8	56.1
Himachal Pradesh	87.4	65.8	67.7	92.5	76.7	78.3	80.7	55.9	57.7
Tamil Nadu	80.1	59.0	66.5	88.1	72.2	77.9	72.2	46.2	55.4
Gujarat	81.2	55.8	64.2	88.9	69.7	76.0	72.9	40.9	51.4
West Bengal	82.0	57.7	63.7	87.6	68.2	73.2	75.4	46.7	53.5
Punjab	78.9	55.2	62.1	83.4	62.1	68.4	73.9	47.8	55.3
Haryana	76.4	55.3	60.9	83.7	69.1	73.0	67.7	39.7	47.0
Karnataka	76.4	49.0	57.0	83.7	60.3	67.3	68.6	37.6	46.4
Orissa	75.9	47.5	51.2	84.3	60.0	63.3	66.5	34.9	38.9
Madhya Pradesh	75.2	40.9	49.1	85.0	55.2	62.4	64.0	25.4	34.5
Andhra Pradesh	70.0	38.8	47.0	79.7	50.7	58.4	60.0	27.1	35.6
Uttar Pradesh	66.7	43.7	46.2	75.6	59.2	61.1	56.6	26.5	29.8
Rajasthan	68.3	37.1	44.4	80.6	55.6	61.5	54.6	16.8	25.7
Bihar	69.7	39.0	42.9	80.1	54.0	57.5	56.8	22.3	26.4
All India	77.4	49.8	56.5	85.2	62.9	68.4	68.9	36.1	43.9

Source: Haque, Lanjouw, and Ravallion 1998.

Table.3: Regional poverty rates								
	Total			**Rural**			**Urban**		
State	**HCI**	**PGI**	**SPGI**	**HCI**	**PGI**	**SPGI**	**HCI**	**PGI**	**SPGI**
Andhra Pradesh Coast	24.05	5.14	1.72	17.07	3.23	1.00	43.45	10.46	3.60
Andhra Pradesh In Nth	18.22	3.39	1.00	13.92	2.25	0.60	30.60	6.69	2.10
Andhra Pradesh In Sth	20.75	4.54	1.44	12.97	2.17	0.50	44.62	11.83	4.20
Andhra Pradesh SW	26.92	6.20	2.25	20.85	4.35	1.40	43.07	11.17	4.30
Assam Hills	38.30	5.23	0.99	41.43	5.64	1.00	3.55	0.77	0.10
Assam Plains E	33.49	6.15	1.67	37.06	6.86	1.80	3.50	0.24	0.00
Assam Plains W	46.04	8.42	2.28	50.04	9.23	2.50	11.05	1.36	0.30
Bihar Cent	51.04	12.54	4.27	53.57	13.23	4.50	35.42	8.34	2.80
Bihar Nth	58.04	14.63	5.11	58.63	14.82	5.10	49.23	11.95	4.20
Bihar Sth	55.36	14.05	4.82	62.25	16.17	5.50	26.51	5.23	1.50
Gujarat Dry Areas	26.17	4.78	1.34	26.35	4.46	1.10	25.27	6.35	2.00
Gujarat East	26.32	5.51	1.59	25.54	5.41	1.50	33.90	6.57	1.80
Gujarat Plains Nth	25.80	4.93	1.43	23.31	3.84	0.90	29.17	6.41	2.00
Gujarat Plains Sth	23.75	5.22	1.69	26.19	5.31	1.50	20.16	5.09	1.80
Gujarat Saurashtra	19.67	3.73	1.18	12.21	2.06	0.70	32.60	6.64	1.90
Harayana East	28.04	5.41	1.70	32.46	6.36	2.00	17.43	3.14	0.90
Harayana West	20.53	4.16	1.20	22.11	4.50	1.30	14.09	2.80	0.70
Himachal Pradesh	28.58	5.19	1.50	30.35	5.55	1.60	9.26	1.25	0.20
Karnataka Coast/Ghata	10.48	1.70	0.45	8.95	1.31	0.30	15.51	2.99	0.90
Karnataka Isle East	19.52	4.07	1.39	14.54	2.59	0.80	37.14	9.31	3.10
Karnataka Isle Nth	42.61	10.80	3.95	37.88	8.31	2.70	57.45	18.65	7.80
Karnataka Isle Sth	29.29	6.11	1.91	29.59	5.79	1.70	28.79	6.64	2.10
Kerala Nth	27.94	6.65	2.31	27.78	6.82	2.40	28.43	6.09	1.90
Kerala Sth	23.30	4.91	1.57	23.77	4.81	1.40	21.91	5.20	1.80
Madhya Pradesh Central	50.46	13.58	5.02	49.40	11.91	3.90	52.72	17.17	7.20
Madhya Pradesh Chattisgarh	44.39	9.09	2.75	44.42	8.58	2.40	44.24	11.52	4.00
Madhya Pradesh Malwa	33.51	7.41	2.39	27.83	5.52	1.60	45.51	11.40	3.80
Madhya Pradesh North	23.50	5.67	1.95	16.57	3.55	1.10	44.14	12.01	4.30
Madhya Pradesh Sth	47.64	12.61	4.61	46.43	11.80	4.20	50.71	14.69	5.50
Madhya Pradesh Sth/W	65.84	22.11	9.90	67.82	22.63	10.10	56.75	19.75	8.90
Madhya Pradesh Vindhya	38.70	8.33	2.57	36.72	7.70	2.30	50.85	12.25	3.90
Maharashtra Coast	13.31	2.41	0.67	15.22	2.50	0.60	12.45	2.37	0.60
Maharashtra East	49.80	10.91	3.54	49.30	10.66	3.40	52.72	12.38	4.30
Maharashtra Inland Cent	52.44	17.51	7.85	49.79	15.91	6.80	61.54	23.04	11.10
Maharashtra Inland East	52.61	14.49	5.46	49.11	11.49	3.60	59.03	20.02	8.70
Maharashtra Inland Nth	50.31	12.52	4.47	47.30	10.92	3.60	58.48	16.87	6.70
Maharashtra Inland W	29.30	6.40	2.19	24.92	5.00	1.60	40.17	9.90	3.60
Orissa Coast	45.57	10.67	3.47	45.33	10.33	3.31	47.23	13.07	4.50
Orissa Nth	43.95	10.20	3.49	45.87	10.55	3.54	32.45	8.15	3.10
Orissa Sth	66.07	18.46	6.99	68.84	18.86	7.06	41.94	15.06	6.30
Punjab Nth	7.64	1.10	0.27	7.32	1.07	0.26	8.32	1.16	0.20
Punjab Sth	16.96	2.89	0.73	17.41	2.98	0.77	15.60	2.65	0.60
Rajasthan NE	22.00	4.65	1.47	17.85	3.46	1.05	33.55	8.00	2.60
Rajasthan SE	35.86	8.52	2.81	33.94	7.92	2.56	42.76	10.68	3.70
Rajasthan Sth	44.11	9.33	2.79	46.30	9.77	2.89	26.59	5.89	1.90
Rajasthan W	24.86	4.26	1.18	25.32	4.27	1.19	23.33	4.26	1.10
Tamil Nadu Coast Nth	41.87	10.49	4.02	44.26	10.47	3.72	38.53	10.52	4.40
Tamil Nadu Coastal	26.05	5.58	1.90	20.80	4.01	1.32	43.00	10.69	3.70
Tamil Nadu Inland	25.54	4.76	1.38	22.15	3.94	1.13	32.02	6.32	1.80
Tamil Nadu South	40.97	10.22	3.71	37.20	8.72	3.05	48.36	13.18	5.00
Uttar Pradesh Central	48.29	13.28	4.84	50.23	13.78	5.01	33.85	9.52	3.50
Uttar Pradesh East	48.11	11.80	3.97	48.78	11.98	4.03	38.62	9.36	3.10
Uttar Pradesh Himal	23.56	4.25	1.06	24.83	4.36	1.08	12.66	3.25	0.80
Uttar Pradesh Sth	68.21	20.28	8.10	67.36	20.17	8.09	74.36	21.06	8.10
Uttar Pradesh West	29.55	6.32	1.98	29.29	6.08	1.85	31.12	7.74	2.70
West Bengal Cent Plains	26.29	5.45	1.70	31.41	6.74	2.10	18.23	3.43	1.00
West Bengal East	45.96	9.77	3.03	47.49	10.15	3.14	35.14	7.12	2.20
West Bengal Himal	55.51	11.10	3.10	58.42	11.56	3.19	32.62	7.48	2.40
West Bengal W Plains	40.82	7.13	1.89	40.73	6.93	1.81	41.78	9.32	2.70

Source: Tabulations from Haque, Lanjouw, and Ravallion 1998.

Table 4: State poverty rates—ranking								
	Total			**Rural**			**Urban**		
State	**HCI**	**PGI**	**SPGI**	**HCI**	**PGI**	**SPGI**	**HCI**	**PGI**	**SPGI**
Ranked by head count index									
Punjab	16	16	16	16	16	16	14	14	14
Andhra Pradesh	15	15	14	15	15	15	5	6	7
Gujarat	14	14	15	14	14	14	10	10	10
Kerala	13	11	10	13	10	10	11	11	11
Haryana	12	13	12	11	11	11	13	13	13
Rajasthan	11	10	11	12	13	13	9	9	9
Himachal Pradesh	10	12	13	9	12	12	15	15	15
Karnataka	9	7	7	10	9	9	4	3	2
Tamil Nadu	8	6	6	8	8	6	3	4	5
Maharashtra	7	5	4	7	5	4	7	5	4
West Bengal	6	9	8	5	6	7	12	12	12
Assam	5	8	9	3	7	8	16	16	16
Uttar Pradesh	4	4	5	4	3	3	6	7	6
Madhya Pradesh	3	3	3	6	4	5	1	1	1
Orissa	2	2	2	2	2	2	2	2	3
Bihar	1	1	1	1	1	1	8	8	8
Ranked by poverty gap index									
Punjab	16	16	16	16	16	16	14	14	14
Andhra Pradesh	15	15	14	15	15	15	5	6	7
Gujarat	14	14	15	14	14	14	10	10	10
Haryana	12	13	12	11	11	11	13	13	13
Himachal Pradesh	10	12	13	9	12	12	15	15	15
Kerala	13	11	10	13	10	10	11	11	11
Rajasthan	11	10	11	12	13	13	9	9	9
West Bengal	6	9	8	5	6	7	12	12	12
Assam	5	8	9	3	7	8	16	16	16
Karnataka	9	7	7	10	9	9	4	3	2
Tamil Nadu	8	6	6	8	8	6	3	4	5
Maharashtra	7	5	4	7	5	4	7	5	4
Uttar Pradesh	4	4	5	4	3	3	6	7	6
Madhya Pradesh	3	3	3	6	4	5	1	1	1
Orissa	2	2	2	2	2	2	2	2	3
Bihar	1	1	1	1	1	1	8	8	8
Ranked by squared poverty gap index									
Punjab	16	16	16	16	16	16	14	14	14
Gujarat	14	14	15	14	14	14	10	10	10
Andhra Pradesh	15	15	14	15	15	15	5	6	7
Himachal Pradesh	10	12	13	9	12	12	15	15	15
Haryana	12	13	12	11	11	11	13	13	13
Rajasthan	11	10	11	12	13	13	9	9	9
Kerala	13	11	10	13	10	10	11	11	11
Assam	5	8	9	3	7	8	16	16	16
West Bengal	6	9	8	5	6	7	12	12	12
Karnataka	9	7	7	10	9	9	4	3	2
Tamil Nadu	8	6	6	8	8	6	3	4	5
Uttar Pradesh	4	4	5	4	3	3	6	7	6
Maharashtra	7	5	4	7	5	4	7	5	4
Madhya Pradesh	3	3	3	6	4	5	1	1	1
Orissa	2	2	2	2	2	2	2	2	3
Bihar	1	1	1	1	1	1	8	8	8

Note: Ranked by decreasing order of performance.
Source: Tabulations from Haque, Lanjouw, and Ravallion 1998.

Table 5: Proportion attending primary school aged 6-10								
	Total			**Male**			**Female**		
	Urban	**Rural**	**Total**	**Urban**	**Rural**	**Total**	**Urban**	**Rural**	**Total**
By quintile									
1	68.01	45.48	50.34	69.52	53.29	56.72	66.47	37.12	43.58
2	79.00	58.16	61.73	80.02	64.82	67.51	77.72	50.57	55.06
3	84.39	65.64	69.09	85.06	71.46	73.89	83.79	58.82	63.58
4	85.44	72.31	74.85	86.60	76.67	78.58	84.35	67.30	70.62
5	90.80	77.18	81.31	91.48	80.08	83.55	90.01	73.79	78.67
By state									
Andhra Pradesh	78.81	58.54	63.69	80.60	64.61	68.80	77.00	52.82	58.76
Asssam	82.66	75.96	76.46	80.70	77.88	78.06	84.44	73.70	74.63
Bihar	70.64	49.12	51.60	72.16	57.20	58.88	68.94	38.71	42.31
Gujarat	84.72	71.07	75.17	85.14	77.31	79.58	84.29	63.86	70.23
Haryana	79.34	69.00	71.50	75.32	74.71	74.86	84.38	62.08	67.40
Himachal Pradesh	94.12	90.09	90.35	92.89	92.22	92.27	95.51	88.01	88.47
Karnataka	83.06	70.80	74.09	85.45	76.39	78.77	81.03	64.91	69.33
Kerala	93.75	92.82	93.01	93.07	93.16	93.14	94.49	92.46	92.87
Madhya Pradesh	80.28	54.60	60.32	81.21	60.28	64.92	79.24	48.16	55.13
Maharashtra	85.45	74.10	77.94	87.45	78.74	81.66	83.50	69.08	74.00
Orissa	70.46	52.78	54.72	71.67	57.19	58.80	69.18	48.24	50.50
Punjab	84.87	78.07	79.98	84.69	79.80	81.17	85.08	75.97	78.55
Rajasthan	71.47	47.95	52.82	76.06	62.76	65.54	65.79	30.21	37.48
Tamil Nadu	91.17	83.52	86.08	91.02	86.94	88.36	91.33	80.07	83.67
Uttar Pradesh	68.40	54.16	55.62	72.02	62.93	63.84	64.28	43.44	45.64
West Bengal	79.99	60.80	64.30	82.26	62.94	66.65	77.25	58.54	61.76
All India	65.26	80.43	61.28	70.31	81.67	67.34	59.56	79.09	54.41

Source: Tabulations from Haque, Lanjouw, and Ravallion 1998.

ANNEX 2: DERIVING THE ECONOMIC STATUS INDEX
From Filmer and Pritchett (1998)

Generation of the wealth index

A major challenge in estimating the influence of the various factors affecting the enrollment decision is a household's economic position, yet the NFHS did not collect information on household consumption expenditures or household income. However, the NFHS did inquire about household ownership of various assets and characteristics of the household's dwelling, and these variables can be used to create an index which proxies for household "wealth" or economic status.

Suppose the enrollment of a child in the jth household is given by host of factors that can for expository convenience be divided into, household wealth, other household factors (parents' education, land ownership), and non-household specific factors of all types (school availability, school quality, etc.). The "wealth" of the household is not observed but a set of N asset variables A^j are. The problem is how to form a linear index of the N asset variables to adequately proxy for household wealth in explaining enrollment.

There are three solutions that have been used in the literature. First, equal weights for all the assets, which has as its only appeal not seeming as arbitrary as it really is. Second, allowing the regression equation itself to determine implicitly the weights for the index by not constructing an index at all but simply entering all N asset variables separately in the regression equation. This approach, while handling the problem of "controlling" for wealth in estimating the impact of non-wealth variables, does not lend itself to easy interpretation of the wealth effects and does not separate out wealth and non-wealth components. Third, one could use the prices of various assets to construct an index of household wealth, which could only be done accurately if one had the appropriate relative prices—which we do not.

In this analysis we implement a different approach, which is to use the statistical procedure of principal components. Principal components is a technique for extracting a small number of variables that best represent the common information in a larger set of related variables. Intuitively, principal components reduces the N asset variables to a smaller number, q, by creating a series of linear combinations of the N variables. The first principal component is created by choosing weights for each of the variables to create an index that captures the greatest amount of common information. We assume that what causes the greatest amount of common variation is a household's wealth, so that an index based on the weights generated by principal components is a good proxy for a household's long-run economic status.

In forming the index we use 21 of the NFHS asset questions, which can be grouped into three types. First, 8 questions about household ownership of certain consumer durables (clock/watch, bicycle, radio, television, bicycle, sewing machine, refrigerator, car). Second, 12 questions about characteristics of the household's dwelling (3 about toilet facilities, 3 about the source of drinking water, 2 about rooms in the dwelling, 2 about the building materials used, and 1 each about the main source of lighting and cooking). Third, a question about whether the household owns more than 6 hectares of land.

An asset index is constructed for each household. The means and standard deviations of the variables and their associated "scoring factors" are reported in the first three columns of Table 1. Each scoring factor is the weight in the index, where each factor weights the variable normalized by its mean and standard deviation.

The average value of the index is by construction, 0, and the standard deviation is 2.3. Since all the variables (except number of rooms) take only the values of 0 or 1, the weights have an easy interpretation as a move from 0 to 1 changes the index by s/σ, where s is the scoring factor and σ is the standard deviation. A household that owns a clock has an asset index higher by 0.54 units, owning a car raises

Table 1: Scoring factors and summary statistics for variables entering the computation of the first principal component							
	All India				Poorest 40 percent	Middle 40 percent	Richest 20 percent
	Scoring factors	Mean	Std. dev.	Scoring factor ÷ std. dev.	Mean	Mean	Mean
1=own clock/watch	0.27	0.53	0.50	0.54	0.16	0.74	0.99
1=own bicycle	0.13	0.42	0.49	0.26	0.26	0.51	0.62
1=own radio	0.25	0.40	0.49	0.51	0.10	0.52	0.84
1=own television	0.34	0.21	0.41	0.83	0.00	0.13	0.87
1=own sewing machine	0.25	0.18	0.39	0.66	0.02	0.18	0.58
1=own motorcycle/scooter	0.25	0.08	0.27	0.91	0.00	0.03	0.38
1=own refrigerator	0.26	0.07	0.25	1.04	0.00	0.01	0.35
1=own car	0.13	0.01	0.11	1.21	0.00	0.00	0.06
1=drink.water from pump/well	-0.19	0.61	0.49	-0.39	0.80	0.57	0.24
1=drink.water from open source	-0.04	0.04	0.20	-0.21	0.06	0.04	0.01
1=drink.water from other (non-piped) srce	-0.00	0.02	0.14	-0.01	0.02	0.03	0.01
1=flush toilet	0.31	0.21	0.41	0.75	0.01	0.18	0.80
1=pit toilet/latrine	0.04	0.09	0.28	0.14	0.04	0.13	0.11
1=none/other toilet	0.00	0.00	0.03	0.03	0.00	0.00	0.00
1=main source of lighting electric	0.28	0.51	0.50	0.57	0.14	0.70	0.99
Number of rooms in dwelling	0.16	2.68	1.96	0.08	1.98	2.97	3.74
1=kitchen is a separate room	0.18	0.54	0.50	0.37	0.31	0.64	0.85
1=main cooking fuel is wood/dung/coal	-0.28	0.78	0.42	-0.67	0.96	0.84	0.22
1=dwelling all high-quality materials	0.31	0.24	0.43	0.73	0.01	0.22	0.82
1=dwelling all low-quality materials	-0.27	0.48	0.50	-0.55	0.83	0.31	0.02
1=own >6 acres land	0.03	0.12	0.32	0.10	0.08	0.16	0.15
Economic status index		0.00	2.32		-2.00	0.07	3.86

Note: Scoring factor is the "weight" assigned to each variable (divided by its standard deviation) in the linear combination of the variables that constitute the first principal component.
Source: NFHS 1992-93.

the index by 1.21 units, and using biomass for cooking lowers the index by 0.67 units.

Each household is assigned to a group, depending on whether their value of the index places them in either the bottom 40 percent, the middle 40 percent, or top 20 percent of households in India. The difference in the average index between the poorest and the middle 40 percent is around 2 units. This difference is equivalent to (as just one example of a combination of assets that would produce this increase) owning a radio (0.54), having a kitchen as a separate room (0.37), having electricity for lighting (0.57), and having a dwelling not of all low-quality materials (-0.55). The richest 20 percent have a wealth index 4 units higher than the middle 40 percent, and this additional difference is equivalent to (again, merely as an example of one possible combination of assets) owning a motor scooter (0.91), or a television (0.83), having a flush toilet (0.75), having a house of all high-quality materials (0.73), and not using biomass as a cooking

fuel (0.67). From now on, purely for expository convenience we will refer to these as the poor, the middle, and the rich, asking the reader to keep firmly in mind this is not following any of the usual definitions of "poverty."

The last three columns of Table 1 compare the average asset ownership across the poor, middle, and rich households. The asset index produces sharp differences in nearly every asset: clock ownership is 16 percent for the poor versus 98 percent for the rich; while the poor use biomass (wood/dung/coal) for cooking almost exclusively (96 percent) the rich only do so 20 percent of the time. One question is whether the asset index loads excessively on variables that are dependent on infrastructure (electricity, piped water) rather than household-specific variables. On this score the clean separation on variables like quality of materials in the household (only 0.5 percent of the poor versus 82 percent of the rich) and having a kitchen as a separate room (31 percent of the poor versus 85 percent of the rich) is reassuring.

Also reassuring on this score is that the index produces very similar classifications, even when different subsets of variables are used. Table 2 compares the classification of households in the bottom 40 percent, comparing the use of the full set of variables as described above with indices based on (1) including only the ownership of assets (watch, radio, etc.); (2) including ownership of assets, housing quality and number of rooms, and land ownership; and (3) all the variables except those related to drinking water and toilet facilities. The classification is very consistent because there are almost no households classified in the lowest group according to the index using all variables that would be classified as "rich" by any of the more limited measures. The robustness of the results is similar for the middle and rich groups.

The levels of the index that define the groups are calculated on an all-India basis so that states differ in the number of households in each group, and Table 3 presents, for each state, the distribution of people across the different economic status groups. For instance, a richer state like Punjab has only 8.4 percent of its households in the bottom 40 percent and 44 percent in the top 20 percent, while poorer states like Uttar Pradesh have 48 percent in the bottom 40 percent and only 15 percent in the top 20 percent.

The fourth column compares these figures with the most recent state rankings by poverty or Net State Domestic Product (SDP) per capita. Nationwide the poverty rate was 36 percent and hence is only roughly comparable with our cutoff point of the bottom with 40 percent. The classification agrees that Punjab, Haryana, and Kerala have better than average economic status and that Bihar, Orissa, and Uttar Pradesh are worse than average. The rank correlation of the poverty rate and the fraction in the bottom 40 percent is 0.794 (p-value<.001). That said, there are differences, like Maharashtra which looks richer (27 percent in bottom 40 percent versus 37 percent poverty rate), and AP, which looks poorer (39 in bottom 40 percent, but poverty rate of only 22 percent).

There are similarly high correlations of the ranking by the percent in the bottom 40 percent group and SDP per capita, where the rank correlation is -0.864 (p-value<.001). Again certain states look different by the two rankings. For example, Kerala looks richer by the index (15 percent in bottom 40 percent versus a per capita SDP of 5,065) and Assam looks poorer (58 percent in the bottom 40 percent versus a per capita SDP of 5,056). However, the poverty rate is substantially higher in Assam than in Kerala (41 percent versus 25 percent), and the percent in the bottom 40 percent is consistent with this, which is perhaps reassuring.

While the first principal component of assets might well serve as a reasonable overall index, one concern with the use of principal components is whether or not the first component contains all of the information. The first principal component explains 25.6 percent of the variation in the 21 wealth variables, which is substantial but not overwhelming. However, there are additional components in the data that do not appear to be just noise. The second principal component appears to be capturing an additional dimension of rich rural households.

This is particularly worrisome because of the urban and rural differences in the rankings by the asset index versus when households are ranked by poverty measures. One explanation is that since many of the asset variables depend on the availability of infrastructure (electricity, piped water, sewerage), urban households are more likely to appear well-off than rural households. On the other hand, this may well imply that standard poverty measures

Table 2: Classification differences of the bottom 40 percent by wealth index constructed from different sets of variables: All India		Only 8 asset ownership variables	Asset ownership, housing, and land ownership	All variables except for drinking water and toilet facilities
Groups based on economic status index using all variables	Bottom 40 pct.	80.24	87.72	95.08
	Middle 40 pct.	19.70	12.28	4.92
	Top 20 pct.	0.06	0.00	0.00
	Total	100.00	100.00	100.00

Source: NFHS, 1992-93.

Table 3: Distribution of people across groups and state level poverty and net domestic product				
	Proportion of people in each group based with groups derived from economic status index			State poverty rate (head count index)	Per capita Net State Domestic Product
	Bottom 40 %	Middle 40 %	Top 20 %		
Delhi	1.3	21.9	76.8		
Goa	5.6	45.5	48.9		10128
Himachal Pradesh	6.8	71.3	21.9	28.58	
Punjab	8.4	47.4	44.3	11.46	10857
Haryana	10.5	58.1	31.5	25.22	9609
Jammu	14.5	55.1	30.4		
Kerala	15.1	63.9	21.1	25.12	5065
Mizoram	18.1	61.2	20.8		
Nagaland	20.3	65.4	14.3		
Gujarat	26.8	43.2	30.0	24.15	7586
Maharashtra	26.9	41.2	31.9	36.82	9270
Karnataka	27.6	52.1	20.3	32.91	6313
Manipur	27.6	54.0	18.4		
Tamil Nadu	32.5	45.7	21.8	35.40	6205
Meghalaya	37.9	49.1	13.0		5769
Arunachal Pradesh	38.1	51.4	10.5		6359
Andhra Pradesh	39.0	40.6	20.4	21.87	5802
Rajasthan	39.7	42.7	17.6	27.46	5035
Tripura	41.8	50.1	8.0		
West Bengal	44.3	38.6	17.2	36.94	5901
Uttar Pradesh	48.6	36.3	15.1	41.55	4280
Madhya Pradesh	49.4	34.3	16.3	42.46	4725
Orissa	54.4	36.5	9.1	48.64	3963
Assam	58.3	32.1	9.6	41.09	5056
Bihar	61.5	27.5	11.0	55.15	3280
All India	40.0	40.0	20.0	36.16	6380

Notes: The rank correlation coefficient between the percent in the bottom 40 percent and the poverty rate is 0.794 (p-value <.001); the rank correlation between the percent in the bottom 40 percent and per capita state product is -0.864 (p-value <.001). Data on the head count index are for 1993-94.

Sources: NFHS, 1992-93 and Haque, Lanjouw, and Ravallion 1998, Agrawal and Varma 1996.

underestimate the degree of differences between rural and urban households by not adjusting incomes for the implicit price differentials for certain types of services created by infrastructure. However for the analysis of education decisions we want an index that captures the dimensions of wealth relevant to education (or health). In any case, the analysis carried out either uses rural-only data or includes dummy variables for rural/urban status, so any level difference due to measurement error should not affect the analysis.

Comparisons with other countries

One question that we cannot answer with the India data alone is how well a classification of households using an asset index would correspond to a more typical ranking based on consumption expenditures. However, we can use two recent surveys in neighboring countries that have both the asset variables

to construct a principal components asset index and expenditures data to compare the two approaches. The surveys we use are the Nepal Living Standards Survey (NLSS) carried out in 1996 and the Pakistan Integrated Household Survey (PIHS) carried out in 1991.

The scoring factors used to derive the asset index for each country are reported in Table 4. There is not a perfect overlap with the asset variables in the NFHS, although in each case the maximum number of variables that were comparable with those used in the Indian analysis were included. In addition we used the consumption expenditures to rank households by total expenditures adjusted for household size, using an adjustment for economies of scale in the household.

The individuals can be assigned to percentiles (bottom 40, next 40, top 20) using either the asset index or the expenditure measure. Table 5 shows the results of the comparison. In Nepal two-thirds of those

Table 4: Scoring factors for the first principal component comparing India, Nepal, and Pakistan					
	India	Urban India	Rural India	Nepal	Pakistan
1=own clock/watch	0.27	0.27	0.31		
1=own bicycle	0.13	0.15	0.18	0.12	0.14
1=own radio	0.25	0.24	0.29	0.20	0.08
1=own television	0.34	0.33	0.34		
1=own sewing machine	0.25	0.24	0.26	0.19	
1=own motorcycle/scooter	0.25	0.25	0.26	0.20	0.28
1=own refrigerator	0.26	0.27	0.21		
1=own car	0.13	0.14	0.11	0.09	0.19
1=own camera				0.21	0.30
1=own jewelry					0.15
1=own gramophone					0.29
1=drinking water from pump/well	-0.19	-0.12	-0.10	-0.02	-0.01
1=drinking water from open source	-0.04	-0.06	-0.03	-0.04	-0.08
1=drink water from other (non-piped) source	-0.00	-0.03	0.01	-0.11	-0.05
1=flush toilet	0.31	0.29	0.26	0.55	0.39
1=pit toilet/latrine	0.04	-0.09	0.09	0.43	-0.03
1=none/other toilet	0.00	-0.01	0.00	0.00	-0.20
1=main source of lighting electric	0.28	0.28	0.29	0.34	
Number of rooms in dwelling	0.16	0.21	0.26	0.24	0.29
1=kitchen is a separate room	0.18	0.23	0.22		
1=main source of cooking fuel is wood/dung/coal	-0.28	-0.28	-0.14	-0.33	-0.24
1=dwelling all high quality materials	0.31	0.29	0.28		
1=dwelling all low quality materials	-0.27	-0.26	-0.28		
1=walls of cement bonded brick/stone				0.28	0.34
1=floor of stone/brick/cement/tile				0.36	0.36
1=roof of concrete/cement/tiles/slate				0.14	
1=no windows/covering				-0.21	-0.22
1=own >6 acr land (1ha in Nepal 10 acr in Pakistan)	0.03	0.06	0.15	0.04	0.15
Proportion of variation explained	0.26	0.24	0.19	0.21	0.18

Note: Scoring factor is the "weight" assigned to each variable (divided by its standard deviation) in the linear combination of the variables that constitute the first principal component.

classified into the bottom 40 by expenditures are also classified into the bottom 40 by assets, and only 5 percent of those in the bottom 40 percent by expenditures appear in the top 20 percent by assets. The classification of the richest twenty shows somewhat less agreement, where 56 percent of those in the top 20 by expenditures are also in the top 20 by assets and 12 percent of those ranked in the top 20 by expenditures are in the bottom 40 by assets.

The results in Pakistan show somewhat less coherence between the two rankings. While it is still the case that only 4 percent of those that are poor by expenditures are "rich" by assets, only 60 percent are correctly classified. Moreover, only 42 percent of those in the top 20 percent by expenditures are also there by assets, and nearly 22 percent of the top 20 percent of households by expenditures are in the bottom 40 percent by assets.

The main issue for the present analysis is how a classification of households by use of assets versus expenditures would affect conclusions about the determinants of educational outcomes. Table 6 compares differences in enrollment and completion indicators between the rich and poor groups when the calculation is done based on either the asset index or expenditures. In Nepal the results are almost identical: the enrollment of 6- to 10-year-olds is 41 percent higher for the rich than for the poor when defined by assets and 40 percent higher for the rich than for the poor when defined by expenditures. In Pakistan, in contrast, the gap in the proportion of 6- to 10-year-olds who ever attended school is 34 percent when rich and poor are defined according to assets, there is only a 26 percentage points difference when the groups are based on expenditures.

Last, in making the comparison with an asset index and a measure of economic status based on

Table 5: Classification differences using economic status index based groups and groups derived from household consumption in Nepal and Pakistan

		Groups based on total household consumption per adjusted household size*	
		Bottom 40 percent	Top 20 percent
Nepal			
Groups based on	Bottom 40 .	65.20	12.63
economic status	Middle 40	29.85	31.41
index	Top 20 .	4.95	55.96
	Total	100.00	100.00
Pakistan			
Groups based on	Bottom 40 .	60.48	21.77
economic status	Middle 40	35.15	35.52
index	Top 20	4.37	42.71
	Total	100.00	100.00

* Adjusted household size is equal to household size to the power 0.6.
Source: NLSS 1996, PIHS 1991.

current expenditures, we do not mean to imply that the asset index is intended as a proxy for expenditures. Rather, *both* are proxies for something unobserved: a household's long-run economic status. Therefore, while it is reassuring that the two are related, discrepancies in the classification of households are not "mistakes" of the asset index and could as easily be indicating limitations of the use of current consumption. Particularly, *current* expenditures would only be a perfect measure under the unrealistic assumption of perfect foresight and perfect capital markets. In practice, rankings based on consumption expenditures are not very stable over time. Misclassification of households, due to the use of current expenditures when long-run status mattered, would tend to underestimate the impact of income for the usual reasons of attenuation bias.

Table 6: Difference between the average for the highest 20 percent and the bottom 40 percent of the outcome indicators using economic status index and consumption based measures to derive groups, in Nepal and Pakistan

	Percentiles based on		
Difference between the top 20 and bottom 40 percent in	Asset index	Household consumption adjusted for size	Difference
Nepal			
Percent of 6- to 10-year-olds who ever went to school	41	40	1
Percent of 6- to 10-year-olds who are currently attending school	42	41	1
Percent of 15- to 19-year-olds who completed at least grade 5	48	49	-1
Pakistan			
Percent of 6- to 10-year-olds who ever went to school	34	26	12
Percent of 6- to 10-year-olds who are currently attending school	33	26	7
Percent of 15-to 19-year-olds who completed at least grade 5	44	33	11

Source: NLSS 1996, PIHS 1991.

REGRESSION RESULTS

All dependent variables are binary and the estimation was done using probit analysis

---

Probit analysis assumes an underlying response function:

$$y_i^* = \beta x + u$$

where y^* is an unobservable continuous variable. We observe a binary variable y defined as:

$y = 1$ if $y^*>0$
$y = 0$ otherwise

The probit model also assumes that the u are independently and identically distributed as normal variates, $N(0, \sigma^2)$, and the likelihood function that gets maximized is:

$$L = \prod_{y_i=0} \Phi(-\beta_i x_i) \prod_{y_i=1} \Phi(1-\beta_i x_i)$$

Where $\Phi(.)$ is the cumulative normal distribution function:

$$\Phi(-\beta_i x_i) \;=\; \int_{-\infty}^{-\beta x/\sigma^2} \frac{1}{\sqrt{2\pi}} \exp\!\left(\frac{-t^2}{2}\right) dt$$

Table 1: Dependent variable—under 2 mortality, urban areas

Category	Variable D	Estimate	Std Err	Pr>Chi
	Intercept	-4.66581	10888.75	0.9997
	Scheduled Tribe	0.14601	0.130045	0.2615
	Scheduled Caste	0.047304	0.077261	0.5404
Water Source- Relative to Body of water	Public pipe system	-0.1488	0.120854	0.2182
	Public tap	0.026106	0.115893	0.8218
	Private Pump	-0.32484	0.138073	0.0186
	Public Pump	-0.042	0.130522	0.7476
	Private Well	-0.35318	0.160852	0.0281
	Public Well	0.026962	0.140962	0.8483
Sanitation Facilities- Relative to None	Private Toilet	-0.05081	0.086422	0.5566
	Shared Toilet	0.019175	0.1154	0.868
	Public Toilet	0.213331	0.104607	0.0414
	Private Pit	0.000231	0.092803	0.998
	Shared Pit	-0.16293	0.153885	0.2897
	Public Pit	-0.00881	0.155921	0.9549
	Electricity in Domicile	-0.02408	0.07718	0.7551
Mother's Education	Literate- Primary not complete	0.037117	0.105253	0.7244
	Primary School	-0.06906	0.080991	0.3938
	Middle School	0.002123	0.088625	0.9809
	High school	-0.16816	0.094641	0.0756
	University	-0.47257	0.136404	0.0005
	Female	4.996386	10888.75	0.9996
Mother's Age	<15	-0.11824	0.08669	0.1726
	15-30	0.001725	0.002632	0.5123
	30-40	0.000925	0.005572	0.8681
	>40	-0.03095	0.035939	0.3892
Decile- Relative to First	Second	0.27552	0.147412	0.0616
	Third	-0.02094	0.148108	0.8876
	Fourth	0.14844	0.13136	0.2585
	Fifth	0.060944	0.134196	0.6497
	Sixth	0.122434	0.129276	0.3436
	Seventh	-0.13512	0.134415	0.3148
	Eighth	-0.03223	0.132168	0.8073
	Ninth	-0.00778	0.137566	0.9549
	Tenth	0.04347	0.151203	0.7737
State- Relative to Kerala	Andhra Pradesh	-0.00857	0.227014	0.9699
	Assam	0.208165	0.194045	0.2834
	Bihar	0.030757	0.207905	0.8824
	Goa	-0.38113	0.243785	0.118
	Gujarat	0.339428	0.193955	0.0801
	Haryana	0.340899	0.210155	0.1048
	Himachal Pradesh	0.174739	0.22817	0.4438
	Jammu	0.387917	0.21537	0.0717
	Karnataka	0.076548	0.194816	0.6944
	Madhya Pradesh	0.171719	0.191179	0.3691
	Maharashtra	-0.03169	0.193386	0.8698
	Manipur	-0.03981	0.31	0.8978
	Meghalaya	0.245241	0.29365	0.4036
	Mizoram	-0.76068	0.40082	0.0577
	Nagaland	-5.0147	5798.339	0.9993
	Orissa	0.335281	0.194405	0.0846
	Punjab	0.228427	0.228599	0.3177
	Rajasthan	0.391293	0.199048	0.0493
	Tamil Nadu	0.243496	0.197379	0.2173
	West Bengal	0.22831	0.213626	0.2852
	Uttar Pradesh	0.255294	0.183062	0.1631
	New Delhi	0.475761	0.181642	0.0088
	Arunachal Pradesh	-4.95887	6546.665	0.9994

Table 2: Dependent variable—under 2 mortality, rural areas

Category	Variable D	Estimate	Std Err	Pr>Chi
	Intercept	0.698364	0.721185	0.3329
	Scheduled Tribe	-0.01252	0.045162	0.7815
	Scheduled Caste	0.107529	0.03592	0.0028
Water Source- Relative to Body of water	Public pipe system	-0.05309	0.067071	0.4286
	Public tap	-0.04866	0.054756	0.3742
	Private Pump	-0.10528	0.053124	0.0475
	Public Pump	0.072689	0.046153	0.1153
	Private Well	-0.15531	0.062878	0.0135
	Public Well	-0.02791	0.045927	0.5434
Sanitation Facilities- Relative to None	Private Toilet	-0.02457	0.083533	0.7687
	Shared Toilet	0.21259	0.181315	0.241
	Public Toilet	-0.08618	0.273614	0.7528
	Private Pit	-0.04987	0.060832	0.4123
	Shared Pit	-2.1E-05	0.145948	0.9999
	Public Pit	0.143233	0.210103	0.4954
	Electricity in Domicile	-0.13791	0.034129	0.0001
Mother's Education	Literate- Primary not complete	-0.07059	0.059142	0.2327
	Primary School	-0.07508	0.046488	0.1063
	Middle School	-0.20964	0.065485	0.0014
	High school	-0.06755	0.07102	0.3415
	University	-0.12566	0.178138	0.4806
	Female	-0.02188	0.287101	0.9393
Mother's Age	<15	-0.14046	0.036736	0.0001
	15-30	0.000151	0.001314	0.9086
	30-40	0.004989	0.002087	0.0168
	>40	-0.00628	0.011095	0.5712
Decile- Relative to First	Second	0.209017	0.048131	0.0001
	Third	0.145122	0.047824	0.0024
	Fourth	0.158749	0.050266	0.0016
	Fifth	0.15032	0.052067	0.0039
	Sixth	0.10309	0.054431	0.0582
	Seventh	0.195753	0.057761	0.0007
	Eighth	0.11117	0.066713	0.0956
	Ninth	-0.02909	0.100845	0.773
	Tenth	0.169527	0.140645	0.2281
Health Facilities in Village	Primary Health Center	-0.11196	0.052324	0.0324
	Subcenter	0.074959	0.034335	0.029
	Hospital	-0.00753	0.047887	0.8751
	Village Health Guide	-0.02766	0.032382	0.393
	Pharmacy	-0.02218	0.033023	0.5019
	Trained Birth Attendant	0.041955	0.030769	0.1727
	Mobile Health Unit	-0.01437	0.042321	0.7341
	Urban area	0	0	.
	Pucca Road to Village	-0.04668	0.029581	0.1145
	Distance to Nearest Town	0.000582	0.000272	0.0324
State- Relative to Kerala	Andhra Pradesh	0.251799	0.117168	0.0316
	Assam	0.260449	0.110453	0.0184
	Bihar	0.204793	0.107546	0.0569
	Goa	-0.23652	0.180198	0.1893
	Gujarat	0.42155	0.11592	0.0003
	Haryana	0.353866	0.121527	0.0036
	Himachal Pradesh	0.193153	0.125897	0.125
	Jammu	0.141996	0.12849	0.2691
	Karnataka	0.137156	0.111792	0.2199
	Madhya Pradesh	0.415206	0.105256	0.0001
	Maharashtra	0.096474	0.12211	0.4295
	Manipur	-0.34294	0.228304	0.1331
	Meghalaya	0.218628	0.150272	0.1457
	Mizoram	-0.56255	0.375269	0.1339
	Nagaland	-0.36461	0.218407	0.095
	Orissa	0.209583	0.113669	0.0652
	Punjab	0.346822	0.123362	0.0049
	Rajasthan	0.220352	0.105974	0.0376
	Tamil Nadu	0.340215	0.121416	0.0051

Category	Variable D	Estimate	Std Err	Pr>Chi
	West Bengal	0.26028	0.108921	0.0169
	Uttar Pradesh	0.385102	0.101283	0.0001
	New Delhi	0.280789	0.255416	0.2716
	Arunachal Pradesh	0.110076	0.155969	0.4803

Table 3: Dependent variable—mortality, ages 1-5

Category	Variable	Estimate	Std Err	Pr>Chi
	Intercept	-1.98078	1.917355	0.3016
	Scheduled Tribe	0.22193	0.090719	0.0144
	Scheduled Caste	0.040856	0.082258	0.6194
Water Source- Relative to Body of water	Public pipe system	0.172722	0.146236	0.2376
	Public tap	0.091557	0.124761	0.463
	Private Pump	0.065085	0.119861	0.5871
	Public Pump	0.232108	0.102442	0.0235
	Private Well	0.182889	0.133578	0.171
	Public Well	0.222295	0.101842	0.0291
Sanitation Facilities- Relative to None	Private Toilet	-0.0059	0.180234	0.9739
	Shared Toilet	0.283785	0.345375	0.4113
	Public Toilet	0.454962	0.394834	0.2492
	Private Pit	-0.3071	0.156438	0.0496
	Shared Pit	-0.29428	0.382099	0.4412
	Public Pit	0.148387	0.433445	0.7321
	Electricity in Domicile	-0.11254	0.075613	0.1366
Mother's Education- Relative to Illiterate	Literate- Primary not complete	-0.49701	0.175769	0.0047
	Primary School	-0.11963	0.096979	0.2174
	Middle School	-0.55712	0.18249	0.0023
	High school	-0.42083	0.184829	0.0228
	University	-0.48585	0.408178	0.2339
	Female	0	0	.
Mother's Age	<15	-0.05492	0.106437	0.6059
	15-30	0.018696	0.004053	0.0001
	30-40	-0.03579	0.038694	0.3549
	>40	-3.11058	13338.93	0.9998
Decile- Relative to First	Second	0.325681	0.108461	0.0027
	Third	0.173491	0.112779	0.124
	Fourth	0.171616	0.117157	0.143
	Fifth	0.254507	0.116329	0.0287
	Sixth	0.211551	0.125806	0.0927
	Seventh	0.132365	0.135664	0.3292
	Eighth	0.206747	0.15124	0.1716
	Ninth	-0.02829	0.243928	0.9077
	Tenth	0.341668	0.322232	0.289
Health Facilities in Village	Primary Health Center	0.006002	0.103483	0.9537
	Subcenter	0.107949	0.073388	0.1413
	Hospital	0.022967	0.09663	0.8121
	Village Health Guide	0.022756	0.069363	0.7429
	Pharmacy	-0.01915	0.069353	0.7825
	Trained Birth Attendant	0.096532	0.065314	0.1394
	Mobile Health Unit	0.098815	0.086667	0.2542
	Urban area	0	0	.
	Pucca Road to Village	-0.01718	0.063871	0.7879
	Distance to Nearest Town	-0.00096	0.001399	0.4911
State- Relative to Kerala	Andhra Pradesh	0.200308	0.275263	0.4668
	Assam	0.583735	0.250004	0.0195
	Bihar	0.053046	0.258673	0.8375
	Goa	0	0	.
	Gujarat	0.735093	0.254191	0.0038
	Haryana	0.368916	0.279623	0.1871
	Himachal Pradesh	0.146693	0.315459	0.6419
	Jammu	0.461263	0.285956	0.1067
	Karnataka	0.260966	0.262225	0.3196
	Madhya Pradesh	0.435299	0.24442	0.0749
	Maharashtra	-0.11025	0.312448	0.7242
	Manipur	-4.87118	6610.513	0.9994
	Meghalaya	0.589252	0.298372	0.0483
	Mizoram	0.849091	0.386602	0.0281
	Nagaland	-4.8154	4737.542	0.9992
	Orissa	0.138665	0.272522	0.6109
	Punjab	0.373867	0.288619	0.1952
	Rajasthan	0.421192	0.239535	0.0787
	Tamil Nadu	0.242699	0.282031	0.3895

Category	Variable	Estimate	Std Err	Pr>Chi
	West Bengal	0.676263	0.245321	0.0058
	Uttar Pradesh	0.440079	0.23599	0.0622
	New Delhi	-4.3027	9061.974	0.9996
	Arunachal Pradesh	0.345099	0.325553	0.2891
Vaccination Card Status- Relative to Seen card, DPT3 reported	Seen Card- No DPT3	0.092276	0.148329	0.5339
	No seen card- reported DPT3	-0.04103	0.102161	0.688
	No seen card- reported no DPT3	0.072611	0.182933	0.6914
	No card- reported DPT3	-0.02698	0.126091	0.8306
	No card- reported no DPT3	0.250836	0.075433	0.0009

Table 4: Dependent variable—mortality, under age 2

Category	Variable	Estimate	Std Err	Pr>Chi
	Intercept	0.873174	0.369767	0.0182
	Scheduled Tribe	-0.07074	0.024738	0.0042
	Scheduled Caste	0.105774	0.018655	0.0001
Water Source- Relative to Body of water	Public pipe system	-0.0327	0.035145	0.3522
	Public tap	-0.00839	0.028573	0.769
	Private Pump	-0.09059	0.027811	0.0011
	Public Pump	0.087325	0.024597	0.0004
	Private Well	-0.15805	0.033812	0.0001
	Public Well	-0.00174	0.024515	0.9433
Sanitation Facilities- Relative to None	Private Toilet	-0.00507	0.042917	0.9059
	Shared Toilet	0.06555	0.100346	0.5136
	Public Toilet	-0.05423	0.138222	0.6948
	Private Pit	-0.06199	0.031741	0.0508
	Shared Pit	0.013707	0.073584	0.8522
	Public Pit	0.173942	0.106772	0.1033
	Electricity in Domicile	-0.12313	0.01781	0.0001
Mother's Education- Relative to Illiterate	Literate- Primary not complete	-0.0197	0.030739	0.5217
	Primary School	-0.08466	0.024428	0.0005
	Middle School	-0.19879	0.034224	0.0001
	High school	-0.09978	0.037986	0.0086
	University	-0.09351	0.091233	0.3054
	Female	-0.04702	0.145411	0.7464
Mother's Age	<15	-0.14704	0.018906	0.0001
	15-30	0.000278	0.00069	0.6867
	30-40	0.004226	0.001092	0.0001
	>40	-0.00404	0.005739	0.481
Decile- Relative to First	Second	0.191917	0.025308	0.0001
	Third	0.122609	0.025059	0.0001
	Fourth	0.132593	0.026334	0.0001
	Fifth	0.145821	0.026991	0.0001
	Sixth	0.080927	0.028495	0.0045
	Seventh	0.170664	0.030062	0.0001
	Eighth	0.09097	0.034761	0.0089
	Ninth	-0.05881	0.053219	0.2691
	Tenth	0.175885	0.073749	0.0171
	Pucca Road to Village	0	0 .	
	Distance to Nearest Town	-0.05971	0.01492	0.0001
State- Relative to Kerala	Andhra Pradesh	0.24265	0.057574	0.0001
	Assam	0.295435	0.054383	0.0001
	Bihar	0.240545	0.052257	0.0001
	Goa	0	0 .	
	Gujarat	0.446067	0.060144	0.0001
	Haryana	0.37531	0.061474	0.0001
	Himachal Pradesh	0.197784	0.064489	0.0022
	Jammu	0.171517	0.063756	0.0071
	Karnataka	0.1387	0.056161	0.0135
	Madhya Pradesh	0.43503	0.05183	0.0001
	Maharashtra	0.046283	0.061288	0.4501
	Manipur	-0.23943	0.112283	0.033
	Meghalaya	0.354369	0.072161	0.0001
	Mizoram	-0.47611	0.187385	0.0111
	Nagaland	-0.3097	0.10937	0.0046
	Orissa	0.31635	0.074112	0.0001
	Punjab	0.350349	0.061219	0.0001
	Rajasthan	0.221666	0.052943	0.0001
	Tamil Nadu	0.340056	0.05968	0.0001
	West Bengal	0.268531	0.053105	0.0001
	Uttar Pradesh	0.394691	0.049535	0.0001
	New Delhi	0.300807	0.126897	0.0178
	Arunachal Pradesh	0.161004	0.077755	0.0384
Instrumental variables	Primary Health Center	-0.00053	0.001726	0.7586
	Subcenter	-0.00474	0.003431	0.167

Table 5: Dependent variable—Tuberculosis

Category	Variable	Estimate	Std Err	Pr>Chi
	Intercept	2.681653	0.078855	0.0001
Decile- Relative to First	Second	0.031476	0.027945	0.26
	Third	0.140082	0.030772	0.0001
	Fourth	0.094835	0.030192	0.0017
	Fifth	0.169709	0.031916	0.0001
	Sixth	0.253352	0.034033	0.0001
	Seventh	0.235971	0.035161	0.0001
	Eighth	0.317147	0.039498	0.0001
	Ninth	0.300414	0.047451	0.0001
	Tenth	0.304959	0.073816	0.0001
Education- Relative to Illiterate	Literate- Primary not complete	0.029604	0.024247	0.2221
	Primary School	0.132862	0.026708	0.0001
	Middle School	0.189775	0.034056	0.0001
	High school	0.278049	0.037037	0.0001
	University	0.44063	0.065729	0.0001
	Scheduled Tribe	-0.01725	0.023305	0.4592
	Scheduled Caste	-0.02035	0.02759	0.4607
Health Facilities in Village	Primary Health Center	0.009604	0.032817	0.7698
	Subcenter	-0.03894	0.023374	0.0958
	Hospital	-0.02664	0.031157	0.3925
	Village Health Guide	0.01381	0.021994	0.5301
	Pharmacy	0.040794	0.022562	0.0706
	Trained Birth Attendant	0.003606	0.020907	0.8631
	Mobile Health Unit	0.069878	0.027175	0.0101
State- Relative to Kerala	Andhra Pradesh	0.194715	0.055743	0.0005
	Assam	0.013216	0.053026	0.8032
	Bihar	-0.00965	0.049374	0.845
	Goa	0.341282	0.069258	0.0001
	Gujarat	0.240788	0.058069	0.0001
	Haryana	0.156089	0.062471	0.0125
	Himachal Pradesh	0.30904	0.069079	0.0001
	Jammu	0.29001	0.069732	0.0001
	Karnataka	0.568635	0.069344	0.0001
	Madhya Pradesh	0.174989	0.050375	0.0005
	Maharashtra	0.233259	0.05791	0.0001
	Manipur	-0.19979	0.064212	0.0019
	Meghalaya	0.207877	0.091736	0.0235
	Mizoram	0.151794	0.092549	0.101
	Nagaland	0.033174	0.080634	0.6808
	Orissa	0.081008	0.05121	0.1137
	Punjab	0.274049	0.065368	0.0001
	Rajasthan	-0.04309	0.046091	0.3499
	Tamil Nadu	-0.03367	0.049773	0.4987
	West Bengal	0.146813	0.056804	0.0098
	Uttar Pradesh	-0.08205	0.043641	0.0601
	New Delhi	0.155254	0.070948	0.0286
	Arunachal Pradesh	-0.17764	0.069315	0.0104
	Tripura	0.2629	0.087222	0.0026
Age	<15	-0.02508	0.002621	0.0001
	15-30	-0.01176	0.001018	0.0001
	30-40	-0.00277	0.000702	0.0001
	>40	-0.00639	0.000916	0.0001
	Urban area	-0.05151	0.024816	0.0379
Source of Fuel	Wood	0.1887	0.053194	0.0004
	Cow dung	0.15915	0.056292	0.0047
	Coal	0.228518	0.076619	0.0029
	Charcoal	0.047578	0.134372	0.7233
	Kerosene	0.187026	0.068086	0.006
	Petroleum gas	0.367487	0.081869	0.0001
	Bio-gas	0.497744	0.173297	0.0041
	Electricity	0.092654	0.144249	0.5207
	Female	0.196205	0.016441	0.0001

Table A6: Dependent variable—Limb Impairment

Category	Variable	Estimate	Std Err	Pr>Chi
	Intercept	2.602658	0.046674	0.0001
Decile- Relative to First	Second	0.016055	0.026988	0.5519
	Third	0.032037	0.027284	0.2403
	Fourth	0.033157	0.027467	0.2274
	Fifth	0.061413	0.028192	0.0294
	Sixth	0.090167	0.028708	0.0017
	Seventh	0.086663	0.029209	0.003
	Eighth	0.109274	0.030095	0.0003
	Ninth	0.150031	0.031997	0.0001
	Tenth	0.222743	0.036202	0.0001
Education- Relative to Illiterate	Literate- Primary not complete	-0.00362	0.022457	0.8721
	Primary School	0.011795	0.023242	0.6118
	Middle School	0.026815	0.0279	0.3365
	High school	0.12453	0.030148	0.0001
	University	0.237151	0.048307	0.0001
	Scheduled Tribe	-0.00026	0.020121	0.9895
	Scheduled Caste	0.042812	0.026255	0.103
Health Facilities in Village	Primary Health Center	-0.03961	0.028297	0.1615
	Subcenter	-0.00871	0.019546	0.6559
	Hospital	0.006687	0.025746	0.7951
	Village Health Guide	-0.04501	0.018603	0.0155
	Pharmacy	0.039871	0.019039	0.0362
	Trained Birth Attendant	0.028288	0.017809	0.1122
	Mobile Health Unit	0.011587	0.022813	0.6115
State- Relative to Kerala	Andhra Pradesh	-0.06848	0.046203	0.1383
	Assam	0.171436	0.05283	0.0012
	Bihar	-0.07141	0.042825	0.0954
	Goa	0.021655	0.050777	0.6698
	Gujarat	0.013272	0.048526	0.7845
	Haryana	-0.08968	0.04981	0.0718
	Himachal Pradesh	-0.05737	0.050221	0.2533
	Jammu	-0.0434	0.050366	0.3889
	Karnataka	-0.09459	0.044062	0.0318
	Madhya Pradesh	-0.03482	0.043332	0.4217
	Maharashtra	4.93E-05	0.047897	0.9992
	Manipur	0.079785	0.073184	0.2756
	Meghalaya	-0.03617	0.073763	0.6239
	Mizoram	0.050895	0.078683	0.5177
	Nagaland	-0.28633	0.063201	0.0001
	Orissa	0.107097	0.047446	0.024
	Punjab	-0.16084	0.047132	0.0006
	Rajasthan	0.015502	0.043771	0.7232
	Tamil Nadu	-0.07203	0.046213	0.1191
	West Bengal	0.193394	0.051077	0.0002
	Uttar Pradesh	-0.04142	0.039904	0.2993
	New Delhi	0.192452	0.061633	0.0018
	Arunachal Pradesh	0.086458	0.079261	0.2754
	Tripura	0.104984	0.070641	0.1372
Age	<15	-0.00484	0.001926	0.012
	15-30	-0.00174	0.00098	0.0764
	30-40	-0.00283	0.000753	0.0002
	>40	0.000941	0.001053	0.3716
	Urban area	-0.31154	0.083687	0.0002
Occupation Class	Prof-tech Low Level	-0.23769	0.06738	0.0004
	Admin/exec/Managers	-0.03502	0.104748	0.7382
	Clerical	-0.14343	0.05508	0.0092
	Sales Workers	-0.08339	0.041181	0.0429
	Service Workers	-0.08312	0.05162	0.1073
	Farm, Fish, Hunt, Log	0.036611	0.028097	0.1926
	Household Duties	-0.07431	0.025083	0.0031
	Students	-0.13066	0.024775	0.0001
	Retired Persons	-0.46114	0.060163	0.0001
	Beggars	-1.26897	0.142343	0.0001

Category	Variable	Estimate	Std Err	Pr>Chi
	Prisoners	-0.37693	0.273359	0.1679
	Disabled Persons	-0.6316	0.025642	0.0001
	Unemployed	-0.47237	0.030895	0.0001
	Calamity in village, last 2 years	-0.03159	0.015285	0.0388
	Female	0.171582	0.016161	0.0001

Table A7: Dependent variable—Blindness

Category	Variable	Estimate	Std Err	Pr>Chi
	Intercept	2.796413	0.032673	0.0001
Decile- Relative to First	Second	-0.04196	0.01745	0.0162
	Third	0.063175	0.018548	0.0007
	Fourth	0.046291	0.018586	0.0128
	Fifth	0.090499	0.01919	0.0001
	Sixth	0.096594	0.019187	0.0001
	Seventh	0.1221	0.02	0.0001
	Eighth	0.139307	0.020206	0.0001
	Ninth	0.133619	0.020787	0.0001
	Tenth	0.226635	0.022838	0.0001
Education- Relative to Illiterate	Literate- Primary not complete	-0.07483	0.013474	0.0001
	Primary School	-0.03278	0.014919	0.028
	Middle School	-0.03799	0.019125	0.047
	High school	0.085395	0.019878	0.0001
	University	-0.01483	0.027019	0.5831
	Scheduled Tribe	-0.03297	0.013729	0.0163
	Scheduled Caste	0.035614	0.016023	0.0262
Health Facilities in Village	Primary Health Center	-0.01786	0.018656	0.3383
	Subcenter	0.019442	0.013565	0.1518
	Hospital	-0.03577	0.018084	0.0479
	Village Health Guide	0.019769	0.012921	0.126
	Pharmacy	0.00376	0.013057	0.7734
	Trained Birth Attendant	0.027636	0.012205	0.0236
	Mobile Health Unit	-0.01272	0.015129	0.4003
State- Relative to Kerala	Andhra Pradesh	-0.83227	0.031938	0.0001
	Assam	-0.11939	0.039668	0.0026
	Bihar	-0.47758	0.032305	0.0001
	Goa	-0.38589	0.035415	0.0001
	Gujarat	-0.49623	0.033494	0.0001
	Haryana	0.108579	0.045567	0.0172
	Himachal Pradesh	-0.0339	0.041268	0.4114
	Jammu	0.099855	0.044925	0.0262
	Karnataka	-0.6984	0.031422	0.0001
	Madhya Pradesh	-0.61919	0.031517	0.0001
	Maharashtra	-0.54942	0.033198	0.0001
	Manipur	-0.21069	0.051837	0.0001
	Meghalaya	-0.04589	0.06697	0.4932
	Mizoram	-0.29751	0.05475	0.0001
	Nagaland	-0.3644	0.055035	0.0001
	Orissa	-0.4597	0.033093	0.0001
	Punjab	0.10156	0.043758	0.0203
	Rajasthan	-0.71105	0.030632	0.0001
	Tamil Nadu	0.196978	0.04186	0.0001
	West Bengal	0.025877	0.039407	0.5114
	Uttar Pradesh	-0.48077	0.030229	0.0001
	New Delhi	-0.32981	0.039134	0.0001
	Arunachal Pradesh	-0.12434	0.062873	0.048
	Tripura	-0.05353	0.054846	0.329
	Aged 41-50	-0.74918	0.013317	0.0001
	Aged 51-60	-1.09625	0.012002	0.0001
	Aged 61-70	-1.44053	0.013394	0.0001
	Aged 70+	-1.71022	0.017168	0.0001
	Female	-0.08536	0.009117	0.0001

Table 8: Dependent variable—Malaria

Category	Variable	Estimate	Std Err	Pr>Chi
	Intercept	3.057118	0.065864	0.0001
Decile- Relative to First	Second	-0.04934	0.014993	0.001
	Third	-0.00251	0.015469	0.8711
	Fourth	0.020493	0.015931	0.1983
	Fifth	0.040846	0.016491	0.0133
	Sixth	-0.00962	0.016281	0.5544
	Seventh	0.048253	0.017275	0.0052
	Eighth	0.110571	0.018742	0.0001
	Ninth	0.105233	0.021453	0.0001
	Tenth	0.183562	0.02682	0.0001
Education- Relative to Illiterate	Literate- Primary not complete	-0.02496	0.011282	0.027
	Primary School	0.00107	0.012632	0.9325
	Middle School	0.010754	0.015528	0.4886
	High school	0.07983	0.017035	0.0001
	University	0.121079	0.028225	0.0001
	Scheduled Tribe	0.015184	0.011971	0.2046
	Scheduled Caste	-0.08399	0.012959	0.0001
Health Facilities in Village	Primary Health Center	-0.06076	0.016227	0.0002
	Subcenter	0.019562	0.01169	0.0942
	Hospital	-0.08802	0.015193	0.0001
	Village Health Guide	-0.00541	0.010727	0.6137
	Pharmacy	0.021279	0.010983	0.0527
	Trained Birth Attendant	-0.02785	0.010205	0.0064
	Mobile Health Unit	0.044259	0.014309	0.002
State- Relative to Kerala	Andhra Pradesh	-1.0015	0.06708	0.0001
	Assam	-1.09764	0.066735	0.0001
	Bihar	-0.92239	0.06668	0.0001
	Goa	-0.39416	0.080336	0.0001
	Gujarat	-1.31834	0.066147	0.0001
	Haryana	-0.79633	0.071163	0.0001
	Himachal Pradesh	-0.83708	0.07074	0.0001
	Jammu	-0.78265	0.071889	0.0001
	Karnataka	-0.48416	0.071625	0.0001
	Madhya Pradesh	-1.41571	0.065108	0.0001
	Maharashtra	-1.35799	0.066147	0.0001
	Manipur	-0.91981	0.075672	0.0001
	Meghalaya	-1.34634	0.070403	0.0001
	Mizoram	-1.36042	0.071248	0.0001
	Nagaland	-1.04109	0.073178	0.0001
	Orissa	-1.38864	0.065327	0.0001
	Punjab	-1.28812	0.067696	0.0001
	Rajasthan	-1.47259	0.06492	0.0001
	Tamil Nadu	-0.57142	0.071164	0.0001
	West Bengal	-0.7263	0.069146	0.0001
	Uttar Pradesh	-1.64768	0.064654	0.0001
	New Delhi	-0.8718	0.073416	0.0001
	Arunachal Pradesh	-1.286	0.071561	0.0001
	Tripura	-1.13287	0.072057	0.0001
Water Source- Relative to Body of water	Public pipe system	0.1067	0.017627	0.0001
	Public tap	-0.01658	0.015783	0.2935
	Private Pump	0.075206	0.016562	0.0001
	Public Pump	0.006916	0.014863	0.6417
	Private Well	0.007762	0.018574	0.676
	Public Well	0.012458	0.014387	0.3865
Sanitation Facilities- Relative to None	Private Toilet	0.136499	0.017901	0.0001
	Shared Toilet	0.187622	0.036043	0.0001
	Public Toilet	0.337708	0.045056	0.0001
	Private Pit	0.088561	0.015731	0.0001
	Shared Pit	0.034165	0.032574	0.2943
	Public Pit	0.115802	0.046102	0.012
	Epidemic in village, last two years	-0.19803	0.010848	0.0001
	Female	0.025218	0.007886	0.0014

Table 9: Dependent variable—Leprosy

Category	Variable	Estimate	Std Err	Pr>Chi
	Intercept	3.569947	0.151627	0.0001
Decile- Relative to First	Second	-0.04163	0.053747	0.4386
	Third	0.049811	0.057266	0.3844
	Fourth	0.0337	0.057211	0.5558
	Fifth	0.086758	0.060822	0.1537
	Sixth	0.127814	0.062237	0.04
	Seventh	-0.0451	0.057985	0.4367
	Eighth	0.097959	0.064444	0.1285
	Ninth	0.266746	0.077787	0.0006
	Tenth	0.183234	0.077064	0.0174
Education- Relative to Illiterate	Literate- Primary not complete	-0.01493	0.042199	0.7234
	Primary School	0.027006	0.046748	0.5635
	Middle School	0.008845	0.056672	0.876
	High school	0.066054	0.05971	0.2686
	University	0.12173	0.094725	0.1988
	Scheduled Tribe	0.036087	0.043091	0.4023
	Scheduled Caste	0.006138	0.053061	0.9079
Health Facilities in Village	Primary Health Center	0.041541	0.065488	0.5259
	Subcenter	0.090873	0.045302	0.0449
	Hospital	-0.04992	0.060659	0.4105
	Village Health Guide	-0.0533	0.038277	0.1638
	Pharmacy	0.023174	0.040631	0.5684
	Trained Birth Attendant	0.071838	0.037678	0.0566
	Mobile Health Unit	-0.13018	0.046718	0.0053
State- Relative to Kerala	Andhra Pradesh	-0.4898	0.158342	0.002
	Assam	-0.22641	0.177928	0.2032
	Bihar	-0.62474	0.150287	0.0001
	Goa	-0.01348	0.209648	0.9487
	Gujarat	-0.15785	0.183126	0.3887
	Haryana	0.049357	0.233303	0.8325
	Himachal Pradesh	-0.24618	0.179205	0.1695
	Jammu	-0.06046	0.209066	0.7724
	Karnataka	-0.58688	0.152552	0.0001
	Madhya Pradesh	-0.56203	0.151504	0.0002
	Maharashtra	-0.4137	0.161545	0.0104
	Manipur	-0.76498	0.16772	0.0001
	Meghalaya	-0.00701	0.303913	0.9816
	Mizoram	-0.21417	0.245037	0.3821
	Nagaland	-0.64853	0.18197	0.0004
	Orissa	-0.38714	0.15763	0.014
	Punjab	-0.2111	0.188281	0.2622
	Rajasthan	-0.58905	0.150246	0.0001
	Tamil Nadu	-0.71298	0.151162	0.0001
	West Bengal	-0.29525	0.165459	0.0743
	Uttar Pradesh	-0.79006	0.146168	0.0001
	New Delhi	-0.62858	0.1615	0.0001
	Arunachal Pradesh	-0.49384	0.193823	0.0108
	Tripura	3.680137	2513.829	0.9988
	Aged 41-50	-0.32084	0.042069	0.0001
	Aged 51-60	-0.32976	0.043903	0.0001
	Aged 61-70	-0.45179	0.048613	0.0001
	Aged 70+	-0.38686	0.074898	0.0001
	Female	0.124687	0.029037	0.0001

ON MEASURING THE VALUE OF INSURANCE WHEN MARKETS ARE ABSENT

Chapter 3 makes the argument that public provision of health services serves an insurance as well as a health delivery function. The reasoning is that private demand for some health services will not emerge, or will be extremely limited, without insurance. Many services are simply too expensive for people, particularly the poor, to cover out of pocket. They could, however, afford actuarially fair insurance for those same services if insurance were available. That is, they could afford an annual payment of the cost of the service times the probability of needing it in a given year. Further, they would be willing to make that payment for the peace of mind or protection from financial risk that such insurance would give. Two reasons are traditionally advanced for the absence of insurance markets: moral hazard and adverse selection. The first refers to the effect that being insured will have on people's behavior that could affect the cost of providing the insurance. In health care, insurance might lead to excessive demand for treatments or amenities that drive up the cost of provision but which are only demanded because the price facing the patient is low or zero. The second reason refers to the different likelihood of applying for insurance given people's own assessment of their need for it. Low-risk people may not buy insurance at a cost that reflects the average probability of needing the service if they feel that they will not need it. If they don't buy insurance, the average cost, based on those who do buy it, will in turn rise. This may lead people at moderate risk to stop buying, and the whole process repeats itself. In the end it is possible that no one would be insured, even though all would want insurance at the expected cost based on their own probability. In this case the lack of ability to buy a desired product imposes a real loss to an individual's welfare.

The government can improve welfare by overcoming this lack of an insurance market. It might do this by providing insurance itself. However, if managing or regulating insurance is too difficult, the government may choose to circumvent the explicit provision of insurance by offering free (or highly subsidized) care. This would eliminate the same financial risk for the consumer as would insurance.

The value of this improvement in welfare can, in principle, be measured by examining people's willingness to pay for insurance. An approximation can be made using the concept of a "risk premium". This concept is illustrated in Figure 1 and measures the amount of money someone would be willing to pay to avoid sudden losses of purchasing power from medical expenses. The figure shows a utility function, or the relationship between disposable income and the satisfaction one derives from it. It exhibits decreasing returns in that it starts very steep and gets progressively flatter—an extra dollar is worth a lot more to a poor person than to a rich one. If you are not insured against an illness, then you can expect to have an income Y if you are lucky enough to stay healthy but would be left with only Y-C if you fall sick and have to pay for treatment out-of-pocket. For a given probability of illness (we'll call it ρ), expected utility is found by adding the utility of a sick person times the probability of being ill to the utility of being healthy times the probability of staying healthy. In symbols this is: $\rho U(Y-C) + (1-\rho)U(Y)$. Note that this same level of utility could be obtained by making a payment of $V+\rho C$ each period regardless of whether you're sick or not, thereby avoiding any uncertainty of income at all. The quantity ρC covers the actual, expected costs of the service and the quantity V is the "risk premium": the extra value attributable to reducing risk itself. It is also equivalent to the maximum amount you would be willing to pay for insurance against this illness, or the amount that makes you indifferent between being insured or not being insured. Mathematically, it is expressed as: $V = Y - U^{-1}(\rho U(Y-C) + (1-\rho)U(Y))$.

This expression depends on knowing what the utility function, U(Y), is. Since we don't know this (and everyone's utility could be different anyway), we need to make one up. The conventional choice is $U(X) = X^{(1-\alpha)}/(1-\alpha)$ where $X = Y$ or $Y-C$, depending on whether the person is healthy or not. The parameter α is called the measure of relative risk aversion and basically governs how "bent" the utility function in Figure 1 will be. The higher is α, the more bent the utility function is, the more risk averse the person is said to be, and the more valuable is insurance.

The value of insurance, therefore, depends on four terms—Y, C, α and ρ—and is specific to both the person and the condition. To construct Figures 3.9 and 3.10 of chapter 3 (page 35), ρ was taken from the 1987 NSS and corresponds to the likelihood of needing inpatient and outpatient care. Costs were also taken from the NSS to construct these two figures. Income was taken from the NSS to be conformable to the cost figures. The average value of income in the lowest quintile of the income distribution was used in Figure 3.10, while in Figure 3.9 income is allowed to vary. The coefficient of relative risk aversion α was taken as near the midpoint of estimates of this parameter made by Binswanger (1980) in his study of Indian farmers.

In those two figures, the value of insurance V is shown as a percentage of the expected cost of providing the service, ρC. This normalization allows us to see the gain in welfare from replacing insurance alone relative to the cost of providing the service. Besides the relationships presented in those two figures, it can also be shown that the value of insurance as a fraction of expected cost also varies with ρ and α, falling with the former and rising with the latter.

This perspective yields several conclusions about priorities for public spending. Public spending should achieve the highest degree of gain in welfare relative to the status quo without public spending, i.e., relative to what the private market would provide. If the private insurance market does not exist, then public spending is worth V, over and above the value of the service itself. Taking only the insurance effect into account, then priorities for public spending should be higher for high-cost items (since $V/\rho C$ rises with C). Note that this effect is the exact opposite of measures of "cost-effectiveness" sometimes proposed as an allocation criterion. Also, the insurance value per rupee of public expenditure goes down with ρ. This means that greater welfare gains per rupee of public expenditure can be achieved by guaranteeing coverage of the rarer diseases. Note that this effect is the opposite of measures of "burden of disease," which are also sometimes proposed as an allocation criterion. The insurance problem is only one of several in the health sector and so does not provide a complete ranking of priorities. It is important enough, however, to cast doubts on the usefulness of methods of priority making which both ignore this effect and give answers so much at odds with it.

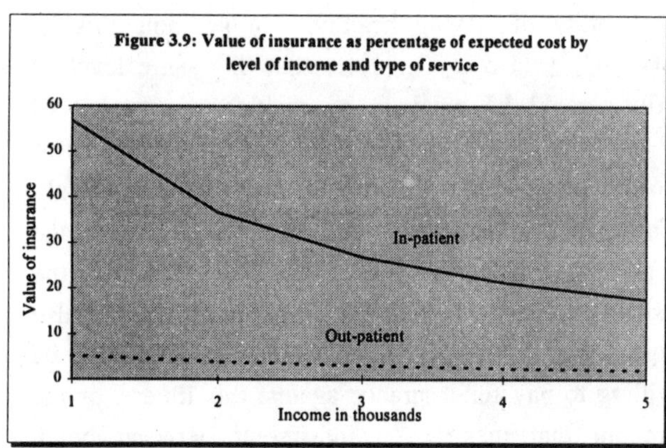

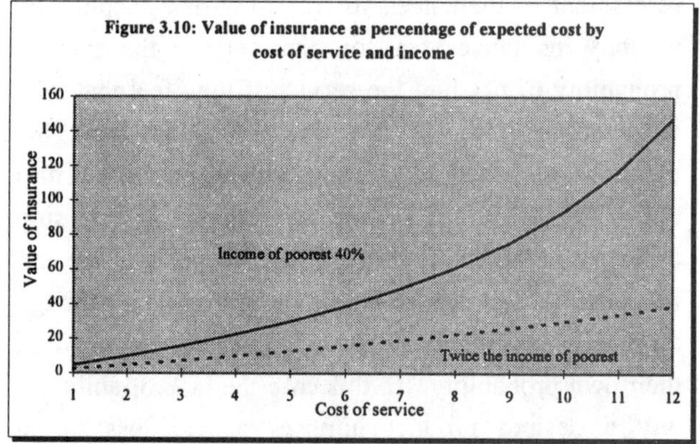

Figure 1

Calculating the value of insurance

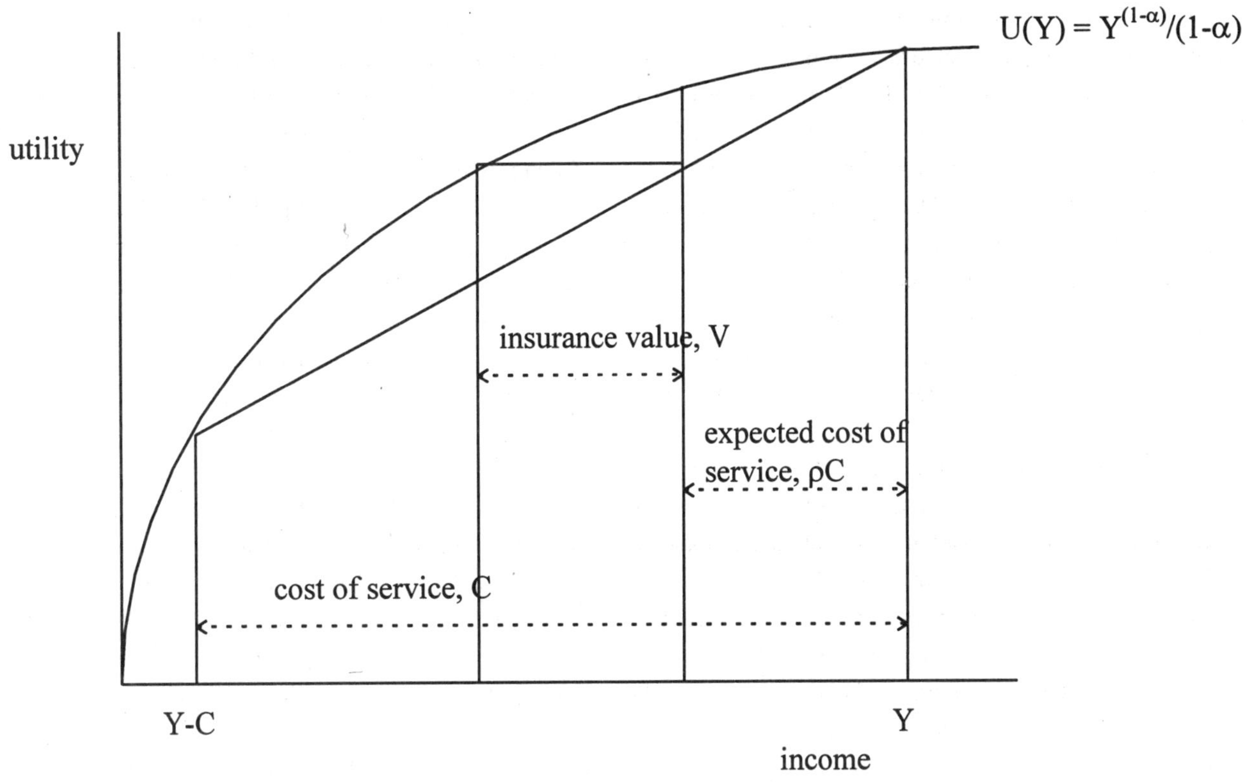

DOES PROGRAM PARTICIPATION REVEAL BENEFIT INCIDENCE?
EVIDENCE FOR RURAL INDIA, 1993-94

From Lanjouw and Ravallion 1998

Introduction

"**B**enefit incidence studies," which are widely used to infer the distributional impacts of public spending, traditionally rely for their key data on a survey-based estimate of how the odds of participation in various public programs vary with the welfare indicator. Typically, the average participation rates for a specific public program will be tabulated against household consumption expenditure per person. A subsidy rate for each category of spending is then applied to the participation numbers to infer the incidence of the gains from public spending and from changes in allocations among categories of spending. Examples of this type of analysis in developing country settings include Meerman (1979), Selowsky (1979), Meesook (1984), van de Walle (1995), and Demery (1997).

Well-established as an important tool in understanding how gains from public spending are distributed, the method nonetheless has a number of limitations. A widely noted concern identified in the literature on "benefit incidence analysis" is that the subsidy per unit of usage may be a poor indicator of "benefit"; unlike commodities obtained on (competitive) markets, the level of utilization of publicly supplied goods is generally unlikely to reveal the value that consumers attach to those goods. For overviews of the conceptual and practical issues that arise in using this method to measure the gain of the poor gain from public spending, see Selden and Wasylenko (1992) and van de Walle (1995).

Another concern is that average participation rates need not be a reliable guide to the incidence of a change in aggregate public spending on a given program or to the distributional impact of a reallocation of the budget among programs. Current distributional impacts will depend on how well positioned different socio-economic groups are to gain from marginal expansions, given the history of the program. The non-poor, for instance, who may have been able to capture the bulk of the gain when the program started, could now be satiated at the margin. In such a case, the poor may well gain a large share of the *marginal* benefits from program expansion even though their share of average benefits is low. Similarly, the non-poor could obtain a high share of average benefits at the same time that the poor bear the bulk of the cost of a contraction in aggregate outlays. For example, see the results of Bidani and Ravallion (1996), who compare the impacts of cross-country differences in public health spending on health indicators for the poor versus the non-poor and find that differences in public health spending matter far more to the health outcomes of the poor than the non-poor.

Measuring average and marginal participation rates

Sampled households from the 1993-94 NSS have been ranked by consumption expenditure per person, adjusted for differences in the cost of living. The average participation rate is the proportion of households in a given quintile of consumption per person who participates in the program. The average odds-ratio of participation is given by the ratio of the quintile-specific average participation rate to the overall average. The marginal odds-ratio of participation (MOP) is defined as the increment to the program participation rate of a given quintile associated with a change in aggregate participation in that program. Differences between the marginal and average odds of participation reflect differences in the incidence of infra-marginal spending.

The average odds of participation are calculated directly from the data. The estimates of the MOP are based on the spatial variation in the 1993-94 NSS data. *First*, average participation rates are calculated for a given program for each quintile and for each of 62 NSS regions, spanning the 19 Indian states covered by the survey. Each NSS region belongs to only one state. The participation rate for a given quintile varies across regions according to the level of public spending on the program in the state to which each region belongs, as well as other variables. To estimate the MOP by program and expenditure quintile, we regress the quintile specific participation rate across regions on the average state participation rate (all quintiles, all regions) for each program. However, ordinary least squares regression will give a biased estimate of the MOP, since the region- and quintile-specific participation rate (on the left side) is implicitly included when calculating the overall mean participation rate across all regions and quintiles (on the right side). To deal with this problem we use an instrumental variables estimator, in which the "leave-out mean" is used as the instrumental variable for the state average participation rate. The leave-out mean is defined as the mean for the state, excluding the region- and quintile-specific participation rate, corresponding to each observation in the data (see Lanjouw and Ravallion 1998 for further details). The following section uses two simple models of two stylized cases to examine in general terms the distinction between average and marginal incidence.

Two models of incidence varying with the scale of a program

It will help in interpreting the empirical findings contained in the report to consider two simple models of how the socio-economic composition of gains from a social program might evolve as the program expands. *Both models posit that the non-poor are able to capture the benefits of social programs, even when they are ostensibly targeted to the poor.* We believe that the government lacks either the information or the incentives to target perfectly, or that doing so risks adverse political consequences—with the crucial support of the non-poor being eroded by perfect targeting to the poor. The models differ in the timing of program capture by the non-poor, an event which will depend on shifts in the costs and benefits of program participation linked to the scale of the program. Social programs invariably impose various costs on participants, in the form of direct cofinancing through fees or more hidden, deadweight losses from participation, such as the opportunity cost to parents of children's time at school or costs to a non-poor person of securing participation in a means-tested program by illegal means. Such costs could well vary with the scale of the program. For an overview of these issues see Besley and Kanbur (1993). For a model with the political economy of targeting in which perfect targeting is not an equilibrium, see Gelbach and Pritchett (1997).

The geography of program placement can also entail scale-related variations in costs and benefits. Since participation costs naturally include transport costs and since poor areas are often more remote and less convenient for program administrators, initial placement will tend to be in less poor areas. When the program is first set up, participation by the poor is more costly than after eventual expansion into poor areas. Thus, there is *early capture* of the program by the non-poor, followed after some point by marginal gains that start to favor the poor with "trickle-down" benefits.

General equilibrium effects of a program could also produce rising costs of participation in a way which differs between poor and non-poor. For example, while a small public works program may well have no effect on wages in alternative work, a large one is more likely to bid up wages and hence increase the expected forgone income of program participants. To the extent that the non-poor enjoy better chances of getting work, they will find the public employment program less and less attractive as it expands. Again, early capture by the non-poor can be expected. Late capture is also possible. For example, it may be far easier for the (theoretically ineligible) non-poor to bribe officials to gain access to the program once its wider availability renders a non-poor participant less conspicuous.

Two generic cases can be identified here. When net gains to the non-poor fall with expansion of the program but are positive initially, then the non-poor will be in a good position to win an early share of the gains from the social program. If instead the cost is too high for the non-poor at the launch but the net gain rises over time, late capture of the expanded program by the non-poor becomes more likely.

The early capture model is illustrated in Figure 1, which assumes that there are just two groups of people, "poor" and "non-poor", with roughly equal numbers of each. On the vertical axis we have the group-specific participation rate in some social program. On the horizontal axis we have the average participation rate over both groups. The figure then gives hypothetical group-specific participation rates as a function of the average rate. In this example, the non-poor capture the bulk of the gains initially, but become progressively satiated. At point A, where participation rates of the poor and non-poor are the same, the standard method would conclude that an expansion in the program would not benefit the poor relative to the non-poor. However, this assumption is wrong since, as the figure demonstrates, the bulk of the gains from an aggregate expansion of the program from point A will go to the poor.

Figure 1: Early Capture

Participation is no higher for the poor at point A, but they capture the bulk of the gains from program expansion

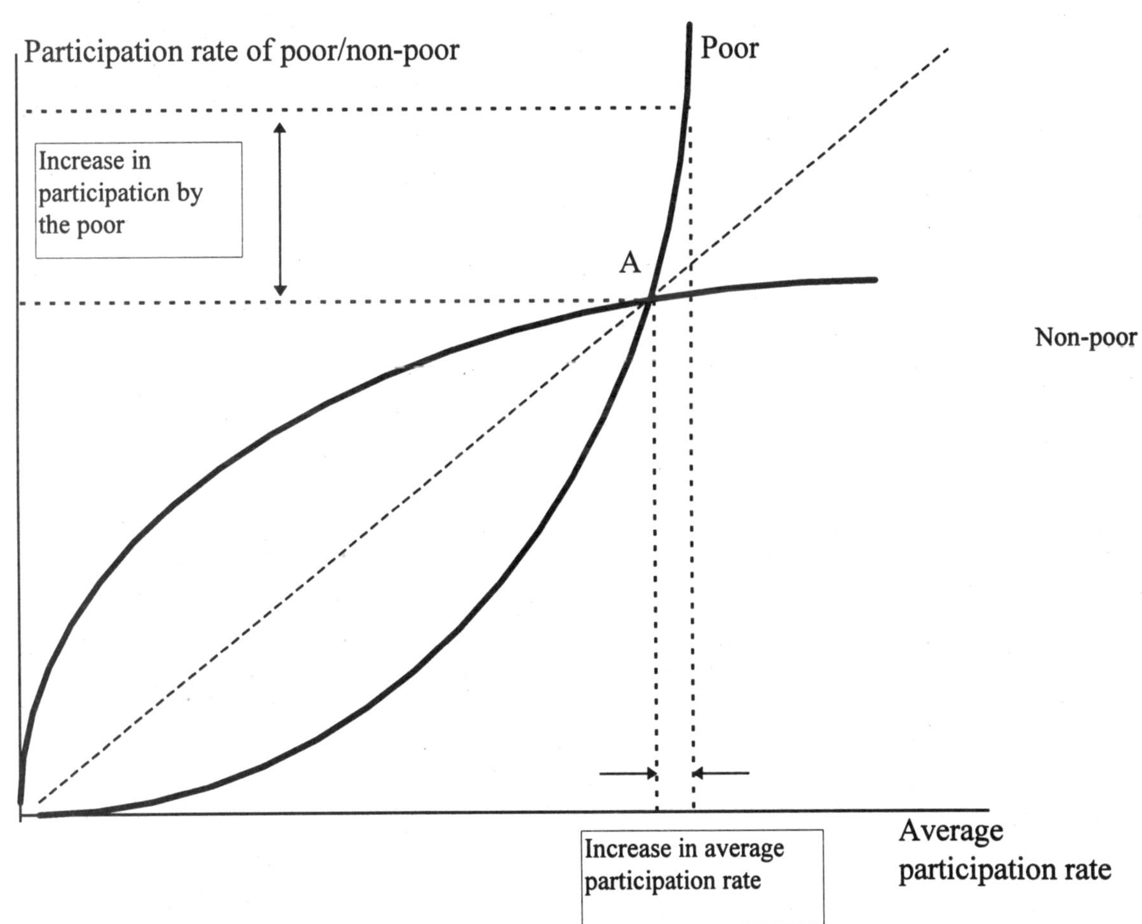

Figure 2 illustrates late capture. Supposing a start from the average participation rate B in Figure 2, the data on group-specific participation indicate that the poor are participating more than the non-poor. Yet the bulk of the gains from increasing the level of average participation to point A, for instance, is captured by the non-poor.

One expects that some public programs will be more like the early capture model in Figure 1, and others will be more like Figure 2. Better-off parents are likely, for example, both to be the first to see their children gaining from public spending on schooling and to become satiated in due course. Marginal gains then go to the poor, as in Figure 1. By contrast, a food-rationing scheme initially targeted to the poor in time accommodates political pressures to favor middle-income groups and thus bestows higher marginal gains on the non-poor—the case represented in Figure 2.

Such unintended consequences of public spending suggest that the average participation rates routinely used in benefit incidence studies may well produce misleading inferences about the distribution of the gains and losses from program expansion or contraction. The outcomes in practice will depend on the specifics of the setting. The evidence for India is presented in Chapter 4.

Figure 2: Late Capture

Participation is higher for the poor at point B, but expansion favors the non-poor

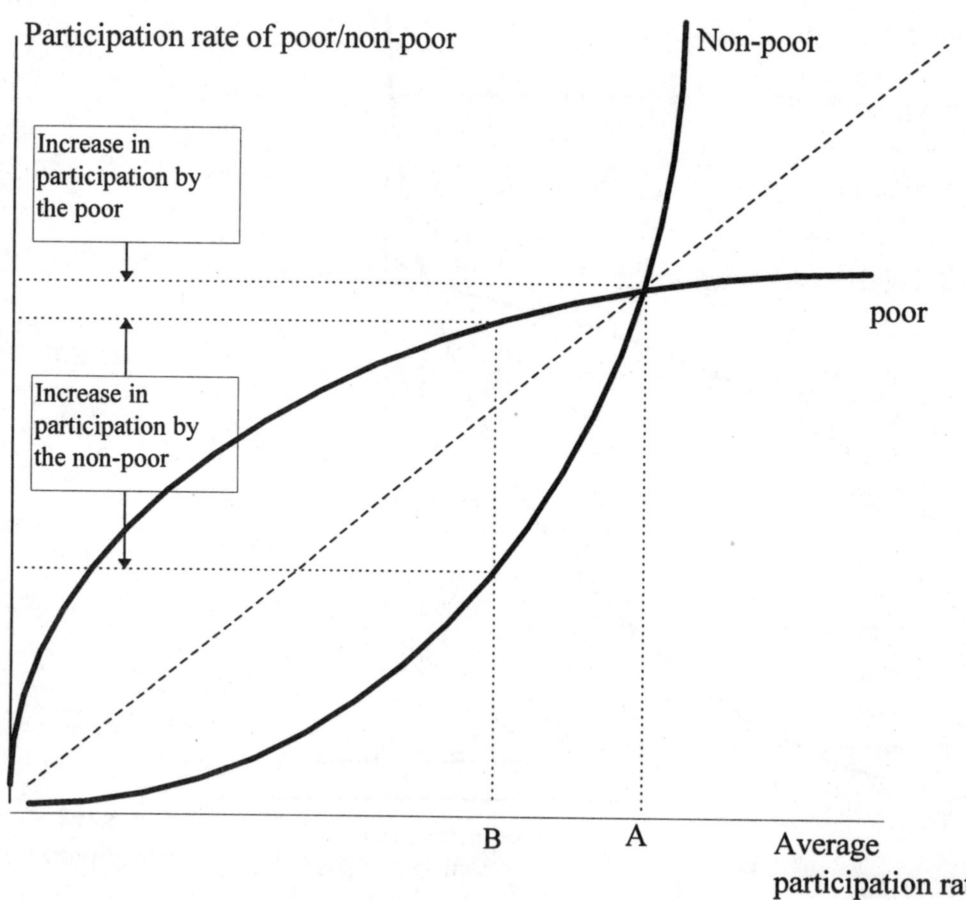

Measuring participation rates for assessing incidence

Sampled households are ranked by consumption expenditure per person, adjusted for differences in the cost of living. The *average participation rate* is the proportion of households in a given quintile of consumption per person participating in the program. The *average odds of participation* are given by the ratios of the quintile-specific average participation rates to the overall average.

The estimated *marginal odds of participation* (MOP) is defined as the increment to the program participation rate of a given household or income group associated with a change in aggregate participation in that program. Differences between the marginal and average odds of participation reflect differences in the incidence of infra-marginal spending.

While calculating the average odds of participation involves a straightforward use of survey data, estimating the MOP is a more complicated exercise. With only a single cross-sectional survey available, as is typical in benefit incidence studies, data can be obtained on program participation across geographic areas ("regions"), within states, or even households within states if micro data are available. Calculating the average participation rates for a given program for each quintile and each region also shows how participation rates for a given quintile vary across regions according to the level of public spending on the program in the state to which each region belongs, as well as other variables which are discussed further below.

To estimate the MOP by program and expenditure quintile, we regress the quintile-specific participation rates across regions on the average state participation rates (all quintiles, all regions) for each program. Our precise method appears to be new. Ordinary least squares regression, however, will give a biased estimate of the MOP, since the region- and quintile-specific participation rate (the dependent variable) is implicitly included when calculating the overall mean participation rate across all regions and quintiles. To deal with this problem we use an instrumental variables estimator, in which the "leave-out mean" is used as the instrumental variable for the state average participation rate. This leave-out mean is the mean for the state, excluding the region-and quintile-specific participation rate, corresponding to each observation in the data. So if one is using the data for quintile 3 in region 5 within state 10, then the leave-out mean is the average for all regions and quintiles within the state, excluding quintile 3 in region 5.

How can the MOP be interpreted? As with average participation rates, analysts must also know the subsidy rates for the programs to infer overall incidence. In conventional benefit incidence studies, the subsidy rate for each program is typically assumed to be one number, constant over income groups and geographically, as though, for example, it costs the government's budget the same to have a poor person participate as a rich person. Under that assumption, the marginal odds of participation can be used to infer the incidence by quintiles of an increase in public spending on a given program.

Sampled households in the NSS are ranked by total per person consumption expenditure (including imputed values of consumption from own production) normalized by state-specific poverty lines. Quintiles are defined over the entire rural population, with equal numbers of people in each so that the poorest quintile refers to the poorest 20 percent of the national rural population in terms of consumption per capita.

In a number of ways these data are less than ideal. The relationship between IRDP participation over the last five years and consumption expenditure over the last month may well be a poor indication of the program's incidence, since participants' living standards may have changed considerably over such a period. "Participation" may also not prove out as an adequate indicator of utilization for the PDS if, for example, the rich buy only a small quantity of the rationed goods. (This conjecture is not consistent with other data on the incidence of PDS purchases; see Radhakrishna et al. 1997.) And there is the possibility that an individual participant may have a standard of living different from the household as a whole; a poor person within a non-poor household may be attracted to a public works project, for example. In the case of public works, it is also likely that the question will pick up participation in public works projects that are not anti-poverty programs as such.

The sample size in rural areas only of the 1993-94 NSS was 61,464 households. The analysis is done at the level of the 62 NSS regions, which span 19 states, with each NSS region belonging to only one state. So in the basic model, for any given combination of quintile and program, we regress the sample participation rates across the 62 NSS regions on the average participation rate (irrespective of quintile) across each of the 19 states.

To infer the incidence of changes in public spending from the estimated MOP requires, as noted above, the assumption common in benefit incidence analysis that the average subsidy rate (given participation) is a constant. For public works programs and the IRDP, the subsidy rate conditional on participation should not vary by household expenditure per person within a given state, but variation between states can be expected. For the PDS, income effects on demand for the rationed goods also could create differences in the subsidy rate across quintiles within a given state. Until state-level program spending data make differentiation possible, we have assumed a constant subsidy rate in this analysis.

PARTICIPATION RATES BY STATE,, RURAL INDIA 1993-94, FOR THREE ANTI-POVERTY PROGRAMS

State	Quintile	Percent participating in public works programs	Percent participating in the IRDP	Percent with access to the Public Distribution System
Andhra Pradesh	poorest	2.3	2.5	79.0
	2nd	2.7	2.9	87.0
	3rd	4.1	4.3	84.5
	4th	3.3	4.4	82.5
	5th	3.2	4.0	81.8
	Total	3.3	4.0	82.8
Assam	poorest	3.6	4.3	84.3
	2nd	3.6	2.8	86.4
	3rd	4.9	2.2	87.6
	4th	2.0	1.9	86.5
	5th	1.7	2.9	84.7
	Total	3.4	2.7	86.2
Bihar	poorest	5.4	5.8	68.7
	2nd	5.8	6.0	77.6
	3rd	4.4	5.0	76.2
	4th	2.8	4.6	78.1
	5th	3.9	2.9	75.2
	Total	4.8	5.2	74.4
Goa	poorest	0.0	0.0	65.1
	2nd	0.0	0.0	100.0
	3rd	0.0	0.0	100.0
	4th	4.6	0.0	100.0
	5th	2.3	2.7	92.1
	Total	2.3	1.8	93.8
Gujarat	poorest	2.6	11.3	84.2
	2nd	4.6	11.6	90.2
	3rd	3.9	8.6	88.5
	4th	2.3	9.9	86.3
	5th	2.4	7.4	83.8
	Total	3.0	9.1	86.3
Haryana	poorest	2.5	7.3	86.9
	2nd	5.1	6.8	93.2
	3rd	2.0	7.3	91.2
	4th	2.1	9.5	90.0
	5th	2.1	6.0	86.3
	Total	2.6	7.2	89.0
Himachal Pradesh	poorest	8.4	5.4	88.0
	2nd	8.2	8.5	89.8
	3rd	9.0	5.6	91.3
	4th	5.9	4.9	91.1
	5th	3.0	4.3	82.8
	Total	6.2	5.5	88.0
Karnataka	poorest	2.9	2.8	75.5
	2nd	4.0	6.8	78.4
	3rd	2.5	5.5	78.9
	4th	2.4	5.1	76.5
	5th	3.0	5.8	78.1
	Total	2.9	5.4	77.6
Kerala	poorest	1.5	3.4	93.4
	2nd	2.9	5.6	96.3
	3rd	3.5	5.2	94.3
	4th	4.2	4.2	94.5
	5th	3.7	4.1	89.4
	Total	3.5	4.4	92.8

State	Quintile	Percent participating in public works programs	Percent participating in the IRDP	Percent with access to the Public Distribution System
Madhya Pradesh	poorest	5.8	9.7	60.7
	2nd	5.7	11.5	66.3
	3rd	4.9	6.8	67.8
	4th	5.2	8.3	70.6
	5th	5.7	9.6	72.1
	Total	**5.5**	**9.2**	**67.5**
Maharashtra	poorest	9.7	7.7	58.8
	2nd	8.0	9.6	68.1
	3rd	8.4	8.4	73.3
	4th	6.5	8.6	77.3
	5th	4.1	5.1	73.3
	Total	**7.1**	**7.7**	**70.5**
Orissa	poorest	9.4	6.2	72.6
	2nd	5.7	5.6	77.9
	3rd	5.9	5.3	83.6
	4th	3.3	7.2	87.3
	5th	2.2	6.3	81.7
	Total	**5.9**	**6.1**	**79.8**
Punjab	poorest	0.0	4.7	67.3
	2nd	3.9	0.5	66.9
	3rd	2.3	6.1	65.7
	4th	2.3	2.2	71.4
	5th	1.9	4.4	72.8
	Total	**2.1**	**3.8**	**70.5**
Rajasthan	poorest	4.2	5.7	62.9
	2nd	6.5	7.1	57.9
	3rd	4.8	5.3	64.0
	4th	4.3	4.0	57.6
	5th	2.6	5.5	53.6
	Total	**4.2**	**5.4**	**58.1**
Tamil Nadu	poorest	2.0	7.5	87.5
	2nd	1.9	5.1	86.2
	3rd	3.0	6.2	89.7
	4th	2.4	5.3	87.2
	5th	4.3	5.5	83.6
	Total	**2.9**	**5.8**	**86.6**
Uttar Pradesh	poorest	4.0	6.4	55.9
	2nd	4.1	7.0	63.2
	3rd	4.2	8.1	62.6
	4th	3.6	6.7	63.5
	5th	2.9	6.7	63.7
	Total	**3.8**	**7.0**	**61.6**
West Bengal	poorest	3.6	6.2	90.2
	2nd	2.4	8.3	91.9
	3rd	1.8	8.2	90.7
	4th	2.4	5.8	90.0
	5th	3.0	5.8	88.6
	Total	**2.6**	**7.0**	**90.4**
Dadra & Nagar	poorest	3.4	67.0	69.8
	2nd	1.7	77.8	73.1
	3rd	5.9	75.0	68.6
	4th	1.0	58.0	71.9
	5th	0.0	25.4	72.1
	Total	**2.3**	**60.7**	**71.3**
Delhi	poorest	-	-	-
	2nd	0.0	0.0	100.0
	3rd	0.0	0.0	48.3
	4th	3.3	0.0	100.0
	5th	1.7	0.0	53.0
	Total	**1.6**	**0.0**	**55.5**
All India	Total	**4.1**	**6.3**	**75.8**

REFERENCES

Ahluwalia, I. and I. Little. eds. 1998. *India's Economic Reforms and Development*. Delhi: Oxford University Press.

Alderman, H. and V. Lavy 1996. *Household Responses to Public Health Services: Cost and Quality Tradeoffs*, World Bank Research Observer, Washington, D.C.

Alderman, H., J. Berman, Lavy, and R. Menon 1997. "Child Nutrition, Child Health, and School Enrollment: A Longitudinal Analysis." Policy Research Working Paper No. 1700, World Bank, Washington, D.C.

Anand, S. and Ravallion, M. 1993. "Human Development in Poor Countries: On the Role of Private Incomes and Public Services." *Journal of Economic Perspectives*, Vol. 7, No. 1, Pg. 113-150.

Berman, P. and M. Khan, eds. 1993. *Paying for India's Health Care*. New Delhi: Sage Publications.

Chaudhuri, K. and M. Ravallion 1991. *How well do Static Welfare Indicators Identify the Chronically Poor?* LSMS working paper.

Datt, G. and M. Ravallion 1996a. "Macroeconomic Crises and Poverty Monitoring: A case Study of India." World Bank, Policy Research Department, Washington, D. C.

__________. 1996b. "Why Have Some States of India Performed Better than Others in Reducing Absolute Poverty?" World Bank Policy Research Working Paper 1594,. Washington, D. C.

Demery, L. 1997. *Benefit Incidence Analysis*, mimeo, World Bank, Washington, DC.

Devarajan, S. and J. Hammer 1998. "Risk Reduction and Public Spending." Policy Research Working Paper 1869. World Bank, Policy Research Department, Washington, D.C.

Drèze, J.P. and A. K. Sen 1995. *India Economic Development and Social Opportunity*. Delhi: Oxford University Press.

Drèze, J.P. and A. K. Sen 1996. *India Development Selected Regional Perspectives*. Delhi: Oxford University Press.

Drèze, J.P. and P. V. Srinivasan 1995. "Widowhood and Poverty in Rural India: Some Inferences from Household Survey Data.." Working Paper 33, Centre for Development Economics, Delhi School of Economics.

Drèze, J.P. and P. V. Srinivasan 1996. "Poverty in India: Regional Estimates 1987-88." Working Paper 36, Centre for Development Economics, Delhi School of Economics.

Drèze, J.P. 1998. Public Report on Education (prope).

Eskeland, G. 1998. "Poverty Reduction and Decentralization." Background Note. World Bank, Washington, D.C.

Filmer, D. and L. Pritchett 1998. "What Educational Production Functions Really Show." Policy Research Working Paper 1795. World Bank, Washington, D.C.

Gwatkin, R. and M. Guillot 1998. "The Burden of Disease Among the World's Poor 1990 and 2020." Presentation at World Bank health and Poverty Seminar. World Bank. Washington, D.C.

Haque, T., P. Lanjouw and M. Ravallion 1998. *A Poverty Profile for India: 1993-94*. World Bank, Washington, D.C.

Hammer, J. 1997. "Economic Analysis for Health Projects." *The World Bank Research Observer*, 12 (1): 47-71. World Bank, Washington, D.C.

India Rural Finance Reform (forthcoming) 1998. World Bank, Washington, D.C.

India Rural Development: Options for a Growth, Poverty Oriented Fiscal Adjustment Strategy (forthcoming), 1998. World Bank, Washington, D.C.

Jain, A., 1988. "Determinants of Regional Variations in Infant Mortality in Rural India," in A. Jain and P. Visaria: *Infant Mortality in India: Differentials and Determinants.* Delhi: Sage Publications.

Jamison, D., W. Mosley, A. Measham and J. Bobadilla, eds. 1993. *Disease Control Priorities in Developing Countries.* New York: Oxford Medical Publications.

Kozel, V. et al: *Determinants of Poverty in UP and Bihar.* Forthcoming, 1998.

Lanjouw, P., and M. Ravallion 1998. *Benefit Incidence and the Timing of Program Capture, Development Research Group*, World Bank, Washington, D.C.

Lanjouw, P., and N. Stern 1997. "Population, Outside Employment and Agricultural Change." In P. Lanjouw and M. Stern, eds. *A Sort of Growth: Palanpur 1957-1993.* Oxford: Oxford University Press.

Levinson, J. 1997. "India Nutrition Program Review." Background Paper.

Lipton, M., and J. van der Gaag, eds. 1993. *Including the Poor.* World Bank Regional and Sectoral Studies. Washington, D. C.

Lockheed, M., and A. Verspoor 1991. *Improving Primary Education in Developing Countries.* New York: Oxford University Press.

Loh, J. 1995. "Education and Economic Growth in India: An Aggregate Production Function Approach." Processed. EPDP Bureau, Ministry of Human Resource Development/Department of Education, New Delhi.

Martorell, R. 1997. "Undernutrition During Pregnancy and Early Childhood: Consequences for Cognitive and Behavioral Development."

Meerman, J. 1979. *Public Expenditure in Malaysia: Who Benefits and Why?* New York: Oxford University Press.

Meesook, O. A. 1984. *Financing and Equity in the Social Sectors in Indonesia: Some Policy Options.* World Bank Staff Working Paper 703. Washington, D.C.

Murray, C. and A. Lopez, eds. 1994. *Global Comparative Assessments in the Health Sector.* World Health Organization, Belgium.

Murray, C., G. Yang, and X. Qiao 1992. "Adult Mortality: Levels, Patterns and Causes," in R. Feachem, T. Kjellstrom, C. Murray, M. Over, and M. Phillips, eds., *The Health of Adults in the Developing World.* New York, Oxford University Press.

Murray, C., K. Styblo, and A. Rovillon 1993. "Tuberculosis." in D. Jamison et al eds. *Disease Control Priorities in Developing Countries.* New York, Oxford University Press.

Pradhan, S. 1996. *Evaluating Public Spending.* World Bank Discussion Papers No. 323. World Bank, Washington, D.C.

Radhakrishna, R., and K. Subbarao, with S. Indrakant and C. Ravi 1997. *India's Public Distribution System: A National and International Perspective.* World Bank Discussion Paper 380. Washington, D.C.

Ravallion, M. 1998. *Appraising Workfare Programs.* Development Research Group, World Bank, Washington, D.C.

Ravallion, M. and S. Subbarao 1992. "Adjustment and Human Development in India," *Journal of Indian School of Political Economy.*

Ravallion, M. and S. Chaudhuri 1997. "Risk and Insurance in Village India: Comment." *Econometrica,* 65 (1): 171-184.

Selowsky, M. 1979. *Who Benefits from Government Expenditures? A case Study of Colombia.* New York: Oxford University Press.

Sen, A. K., and S. Sengupta 1983. "Malnutrition of rural Children and the Sex Bias." *Economic and Political Weekly* 18: 855-64.

Srinivasan, K. 1998. "Some Issues in the Selection and Assessment of the Determinants of Infant Mortality." In A. Jain and P. Visaria, eds., *Infant Mortality in India: Differentials and Determinants.* New Delhi: Sage Publications.

Srivastava, N. 1998. "Only God Can Help Them. Understanding the Multiple Dimensions of Rural Poverty." Background paper.

Srivastava, R. 1988. "Devolution in India Since the 73rd Amendment Implications for Safety Nets and the social Sector." Background paper.

Stiglitz, J. 1995. "Role of Government in the Contemporary World." Preliminary draft. International Monetary Fund, Washington, D.C.

Subbarao, K., A. Bonnerjee, J. Braithwaite, S. Carvalho, K. Ezemenari, C. Graham, and A. Thompson 1997. *Safety Net Programs and Poverty Reduction.* World Bank, Washington, D.C.

Townsend 1991. Risk and Insurance in Village India, as reported in Adjustment and human development in India.

Unni, J. 1997. Non-Agricultural Employment and Rural Livelihoods. Background Paper.

van de Walle, D., and K. Nead 1995. *Public spending and the Poor.* The Johns Hopkins University Press.

van de Walle, D. 1998. "Assessing the Welfare Impacts of Public Spending." *World Development,* 26(3).

van der Gaag, J. 1996. Early Child Development: *An Economic Perspective.* Published by: Elsevier Science B.V. Netherlands.

World Bank, 1990. *World Development Report 1990: Poverty.* New York: Oxford University Press.

World Bank, 1993. *World Development Report 1993: Investing in Health.* New York: Oxford University Press.

World Bank, 1995a. *India's Family Welfare Program: Toward a Reproductive and Child Health Approach.* Report No. 14644-IN, Washington, D.C.

World Bank, 1995b. *India: Policy and Finance Strategies for Strengthening Primary Health Care Services.* Washington, D.C.

World Bank, 1996. *India: Five Years of Stabilization and Reform and the Challenges Ahead.* Washington, D.C.

World Bank, 1997. *World Development Report 1997: The State in a Changing World.* New York: Oxford University Press.

World Bank, 1997a. *Primary Education in India.* Development in Practice series, Washington, D.C.

__________ 1997b. *India Achievements and Challenges in Reducing Poverty.* A World Bank Country Study, Washington, D.C.

__________, 1997c. *India Sustaining Rapid Economic Growth.* Country Economic Memorandum, Washington, D.C.

__________, 1997d. *India New Directions in Health Sector Development at the State Level: An Operational Prospective.* Report 15753-IN, Washington, D.C.

__________, 1997e. *Health, Nutrition and Population*, World Bank, Washington, D.C.

__________, 1998f. *Reforming for Growth and Poverty Reduction* (forthcoming). World Bank. Washington, D.C.

Young, M., ed. 1996. Early Child Development*: Investing in Our Children's Future.* Published by: Elsevier Science B.V. Netherlands.

Distributors of World Bank Publications

Prices and credit terms vary from country to country. Consult your local distributor before placing an order.

ARGENTINA
Oficina del Libro Internacional
Av. Cordoba 1877
1120 Buenos Aires
Tel: (54 1) 815-8354
Fax: (54 1) 815-8156
E-mail: olilibro@satlink.com

AUSTRALIA, FIJI, PAPUA NEW GUINEA, SOLOMON ISLANDS, VANUATU, AND SAMOA
D.A. Information Services
648 Whitehorse Road
Mitcham 3132
Victoria
Tel: (61) 3 9210 7777
Fax: (61) 3 9210 7788
E-mail: service@dadirect.com.au

AUSTRIA
Gerold and Co.
Weihburggasse 26
A-1011 Wien
Tel: (43 1) 512-47-31-0
Fax: (43 1) 512-47-31-29

BANGLADESH
Micro Industries Development
   Assistance Society (MIDAS)
House 5, Road 16
Dhanmondi R/Area
Dhaka 1209
Tel: (880 2) 326427
Fax: (880 2) 811188

BELGIUM
Jean De Lannoy
Av. du Roi 202
1060 Brussels
Tel: (32 2) 538-5169
Fax: (32 2) 538-0841

BRAZIL
Publicacões Tecnicas Internacionais Ltda.
Rua Peixoto Gomide, 209
01409 Sao Paulo, SP.
Tel: (55 11) 259-6644
Fax: (55 11) 258-6990
E-mail: postmaster@pti.uol.br

CANADA
Renouf Publishing Co. Ltd.
5369 Canotek Road
Ottawa, Ontario K1J 9J3
Tel: (613) 745-2665
Fax: (613) 745-7660
E-mail: order.dept@renoufbooks.com

CHINA
China Financial & Economic
Publishing House
8, Da Fo Si Dong Jie
Beijing
Tel: (86 10) 6333-8257
Fax: (86 10) 6401-7365

China Book Import Centre
P.O. Box 2825
Beijing

COLOMBIA
Infoenlace Ltda.
Carrera 6 No. 51-21
Apartado Aereo 34270
Santafé de Bogotá, D.C.
Tel: (57 1) 285-2798
Fax: (57 1) 285-2798

COTE D'IVOIRE
Center d'Edition et de Diffusion Africaines
(CEDA)
04 B.P. 541
Abidjan 04
Tel: (225) 24 6510; 24 6511
Fax: (225) 25 0567

CYPRUS
Center for Applied Research
Cyprus College
6, Diogenes Street, Engomi
P.O. Box 2006
Nicosia
Tel: (357 2) 44-1730
Fax: (357 2) 46-2051

CZECH REPUBLIC
USIS, NIS Prodejna
Havelkova 22
130 00 Prague 3
Tel: (420 2) 2423 1486
Fax: (420 2) 2423 1114

DENMARK
SamfundsLitteratur
Rosenoerns Allé 11
DK-1970 Frederiksberg C
Tel: (45 31) 351942
Fax: (45 31) 357822

ECUADOR
Libri Mundi
Libreria Internacional
P.O. Box 17-01-3029
Juan Leon Mera 851
Quito
Tel: (593 2) 521-606; (593 2) 544-185
Fax: (593 2) 504-209
E-mail: librimu1@librimundi.com.ec

CODEU
Ruiz de Castilla 763, Edif. Expocolor
Primer piso, Of. #2
Quito
Tel/Fax: (593 2) 507-383; 253-091
E-mail: codeu@impsat.net.ec

EGYPT, ARAB REPUBLIC OF
Al Ahram Distribution Agency
Al Galaa Street
Cairo
Tel: (20 2) 578-6083
Fax: (20 2) 578-6833

The Middle East Observer
41, Sherif Street
Cairo
Tel: (20 2) 393-9732
Fax: (20 2) 393-9732

FINLAND
Akateeminen Kirjakauppa
P.O. Box 128
FIN-00101 Helsinki
Tel: (358 0) 121 4418
Fax: (358 0) 121-4435
E-mail: akatilaus@stockmann.fi

FRANCE
World Bank Publications
66, avenue d'Iéna
75116 Paris
Tel: (33 1) 40-69-30-56/57
Fax: (33 1) 40-69-30-68

GERMANY
UNO-Verlag
Poppelsdorfer Allee 55
53115 Bonn
Tel: (49 228) 949020
Fax: (49 228) 217492
E-mail: unoverlag@aol.com

GHANA
Epp Books Services
P.O. Box 44
TUC
Accra

GREECE
Papasotiriou S.A.
35, Stoumara Str.
106 82 Athens
Tel: (30 1) 364-1826
Fax: (30 1) 364-8254

HAITI
Culture Diffusion
5, Rue Capois
C.P. 257
Port-au-Prince
Tel: (509) 23 9260
Fax: (509) 23 4858

HONG KONG, CHINA; MACAO
Asia 2000 Ltd.
Sales & Circulation Department
Seabird House, unit 1101-02
22-28 Wyndham Street, Central
Hong Kong
Tel: (852) 2530-1409
Fax: (852) 2526-1107
E-mail: sales@asia2000.com.hk

HUNGARY
Euro Info Service
Margitszgeti Europa Haz
H-1138 Budapest
Tel: (36 1) 350 80 24, 350 80 25
Fax: (36 1) 350 90 32
E-mail: euroinfo@mail.matav.hu

INDIA
Allied Publishers Ltd.
751 Mount Road
Madras - 600 002
Tel: (91 44) 852-3938
Fax: (91 44) 852-0649

INDONESIA
Pt. Indira Limited
Jalan Borobudur 20
P.O. Box 181
Jakarta 10320
Tel: (62 21) 390-4290
Fax: (62 21) 390-4289

IRAN
Ketab Sara Co. Publishers
Khaled Eslamboli Ave., 6th Street
Delafrooz Alley No. 8
P.O. Box 15745-733
Tehran 15117
Tel: (98 21) 8717819; 8716104
Fax: (98 21) 8712479
E-mail: ketab-sara@neda.net.ir

Kowkab Publishers
P.O. Box 19575-511
Tehran
Tel: (98 21) 258-3723
Fax: (98 21) 258-3723

IRELAND
Government Supplies Agency
Oifig an tSoláthair
4-5 Harcourt Road
Dublin 2
Tel: (353 1) 661-3111
Fax: (353 1) 475-2670

ISRAEL
Yozmot Literature Ltd.
P.O. Box 56055
3 Yohanan Hasandlar Street
Tel Aviv 61560
Tel: (972 3) 5285-397
Fax: (972 3) 5285-397

R.O.Y. International
PO Box 13056
Tel Aviv 61130
Tel: (972 3) 5461423
Fax: (972 3) 5461442
E-mail: royil@netvision.net.il

Palestinian Authority/Middle East
Index Information Services
P.O.B. 19502 Jerusalem
Tel: (972 2) 6271219
Fax: (972 2) 6271634

ITALY
Licosa Commissionaria Sansoni SPA
Via Duca Di Calabria, 1/1
Casella Postale 552
50125 Firenze
Tel: (55) 645-415
Fax: (55) 641-257
E-mail: licosa@ftbcc.it

JAMAICA
Ian Randle Publishers Ltd.
206 Old Hope Road, Kingston 6
Tel: 876-927-2085
Fax: 876-977-0243
E-mail: irpl@colis.com

JAPAN
Eastern Book Service
3-13 Hongo 3-chome, Bunkyo-ku
Tokyo 113
Tel: (81 3) 3818-0861
Fax: (81 3) 3818-0864
E-mail: orders@svt-ebs.co.jp

KENYA
Africa Book Service (E.A.) Ltd.
Quaran House, Mfangano Street
P.O. Box 45245
Nairobi
Tel: (254 2) 223 641
Fax: (254 2) 330 272

KOREA, REPUBLIC OF
Daejon Trading Co. Ltd.
P.O. Box 34, Youida, 706 Seoun Bldg
44-6 Youido-Dong, Yeongchengpo-Ku
Seoul
Tel: (82 2) 785-1631/4
Fax: (82 2) 784-0315

LEBANON
Librairie du Liban
P.O. Box 11-9232
Beirut
Tel: (961 9) 217 944
Fax: (961 9) 217 434

MALAYSIA
University of Malaya Cooperative
   Bookshop, Limited
P.O. Box 1127
Jalan Pantai Baru
59700 Kuala Lumpur
Tel: (60 3) 756-5000
Fax: (60 3) 755-4424
E-mail: umkoop@tm.net.my

MEXICO
INFOTEC
Av. San Fernando No. 37
Col. Toriello Guerra
14050 Mexico, D.F.
Tel: (52 5) 624-2800
Fax: (52 5) 624-2822
E-mail: infotec@rtn.net.mx

Mundi-Prensa Mexico S.A. de C.V.
c/Rio Panuco, 141-Colonia Cuauhtemoc
06500 Mexico, D.F.
Tel: (52 5) 533-5658
Fax: (52 5) 514-6799

NEPAL
Everest Media International Services (P.) Ltd.
GPO Box 5443
Kathmandu
Tel: (977 1) 472 152
Fax: (977 1) 224 431

NETHERLANDS
De Lindeboom/InOr-Publikaties
P.O. Box 202, 7480 AE Haaksbergen
Tel: (31 53) 574-0004
Fax: (31 53) 572-9296
E-mail: lindeboo@worldonline.nl

NEW ZEALAND
EBSCO NZ Ltd.
Private Mail Bag 99914
New Market
Auckland
Tel: (64 9) 524-8119
Fax: (64 9) 524-8067

NIGERIA
University Press Limited
Three Crowns Building Jericho
Private Mail Bag 5095
Ibadan
Tel: (234 22) 41-1356
Fax: (234 22) 41-2056

NORWAY
NIC Info A/S
Book Department, Postboks 6512 Etterstad
N-0606 Oslo
Tel: (47 22) 97-4500
Fax: (47 22) 97-4545

PAKISTAN
Mirza Book Agency
65, Shahrah-e-Quaid-e-Azam
Lahore 54000
Tel: (92 42) 735 3601
Fax: (92 42) 576 3714

Oxford University Press
5 Bangalore Town
Sharae Faisal
PO Box 13033
Karachi-75350
Tel: (92 21) 446307
Fax: (92 21) 4547640
E-mail: ouppak@TheOffice.net

Pak Book Corporation
Aziz Chambers 21, Queen's Road
Lahore
Tel: (92 42) 636 3222; 636 0885
Fax: (92 42) 636 2328
E-mail: pbc@brain.net.pk

PERU
Editorial Desarrollo SA
Apartado 3824, Lima 1
Tel: (51 14) 285380
Fax: (51 14) 286628

PHILIPPINES
International Booksource Center Inc.
1127-A Antipolo St, Barangay, Venezuela
Makati City
Tel: (63 2) 896 6501; 6505; 6507
Fax: (63 2) 896 1741

POLAND
International Publishing Service
Ul. Piekna 31/37
00-677 Warzawa
Tel: (48 2) 628-6089
Fax: (48 2) 621-7255
E-mail: books%ips@ikp.atm.com.pl

PORTUGAL
Livraria Portugal
Apartado 2681, Rua Do Carmo 70-74
1200 Lisbon
Tel: (1) 347-4982
Fax: (1) 347-0264

ROMANIA
Compani De Librarii Bucuresti S.A.
Str. Lipscani no. 26, sector 3
Bucharest
Tel: (40 1) 613 9645
Fax: (40 1) 312 4000

RUSSIAN FEDERATION
Isdatelstvo <Ves Mir>
9a, Kolpachniy Pereulok
Moscow 101831
Tel: (7 095) 917 87 49
Fax: (7 095) 917 92 59

SINGAPORE; TAIWAN, CHINA; MYANMAR; BRUNEI
Ashgate Publishing Asia Pacific Pte. Ltd.
41 Kallang Pudding Road #04-03
Golden Wheel Building
Singapore 349316
Tel: (65) 741-5166
Fax: (65) 742-9356
E-mail: ashgate@asianconnect.com

SLOVENIA
Gospodarski Vestnik Publishing Group
Dunajska cesta 5
1000 Ljubljana
Tel: (386 61) 133 83 47; 132 12 30
Fax: (386 61) 133 80 30
E-mail: repansekj@gvestnik.si

SOUTH AFRICA, BOTSWANA
For single titles:
Oxford University Press Southern Africa
Vasco Boulevard, Goodwood
P.O. Box 12119, N1 City 7463
Cape Town
Tel: (27 21) 595 4400
Fax: (27 21) 595 4430
E-mail: oxford@oup.co.za

For subscription orders:
International Subscription Service
P.O. Box 41095
Craighall
Johannesburg 2024
Tel: (27 11) 880-1448
Fax: (27 11) 880-6248
E-mail: iss@is.co.za

SPAIN
Mundi-Prensa Libros, S.A.
Castello 37
28001 Madrid
Tel: (34 1) 431-3399
Fax: (34 1) 575-3998
E-mail: libreria@mundiprensa.es

Mundi-Prensa Barcelona
Consell de Cent, 391
08009 Barcelona
Tel: (34 3) 488-3492
Fax: (34 3) 487-7659
E-mail: barcelona@mundiprensa.es

SRI LANKA, THE MALDIVES
Lake House Bookshop
100, Sir Chittampalam Gardiner Mawatha
Colombo 2
Tel: (94 1) 32105
Fax: (94 1) 432104
E-mail: LHL@sri.lanka.net

SWEDEN
Wennergren-Williams AB
P.O. Box 1305
S-171 25 Solna
Tel: (46 8) 705-97-50
Fax: (46 8) 27-00-71
E-mail: mail@wwi.se

SWITZERLAND
Librairie Payot Service Institutionnel
Côtes-de-Montbenon 30
1002 Lausanne
Tel: (41 21) 341-3229
Fax: (41 21) 341-3235

ADECO Van Diermen EditionsTechniques
Ch. de Lacuez 41
CH1807 Blonay
Tel: (41 21) 943 2673
Fax: (41 21) 943 3605

THAILAND
Central Books Distribution
306 Silom Road
Bangkok 10500
Tel: (66 2) 235-5400
Fax: (66 2) 237-8321

TRINIDAD & TOBAGO AND THE CARRIBBEAN
Systematics Studies Ltd.
St. Augustine Shopping Center
Eastern Main Road, St. Augustine
Trinidad & Tobago, West Indies
Tel: (868) 645-8466
Fax: (868) 645-8467
E-mail: tobe@trinidad.net

UGANDA
Gustro Ltd.
PO Box 9997, Madhvani Building
Plot 16/4 Jinja Rd.
Kampala
Tel: (256 41) 251 467
Fax: (256 41) 251 468
E-mail: gus@swiftuganda.com

UNITED KINGDOM
Microinfo Ltd.
P.O. Box 3, Alton, Hampshire GU34 2PG
England
Tel: (44 1420) 86848
Fax: (44 1420) 89889
E-mail: wbank@ukminfo.demon.co.uk

The Stationery Office
51 Nine Elms Lane
London SW8 5DR
Tel: (44 171) 873-8400
Fax: (44 171) 873-8242

VENEZUELA
Tecni-Ciencia Libros, S.A.
Centro Cuidad Comercial Tamanco
Nivel C2, Caracas
Tel: (58 2) 959 5547; 5035; 0016
Fax: (58 2) 959 5636

ZAMBIA
University Bookshop, University of Zambia
Great East Road Campus
P.O. Box 32379
Lusaka
Tel: (260 1) 252 576
Fax: (260 1) 253 952

ZIMBABWE
Academic and Baobab Books (Pvt.) Ltd.
4 Conald Road, Graniteside
P.O. Box 567
Harare
Tel: 263 4 755035
Fax: 263 4 781913